GIVING THE EXCHANGE

A COURSE IN RELATIONAL EVANGELISM AND DISCIPLESHIP

JEFF MUSGRAVE

Greenville, South Carolina

The fact that materials produced by other publishers may be referred to in this volume does not constitute an endorsement of the content or theological position of materials produced by such publishers.

All Scripture is quoted from the Authorized King James Version. Emphasis in bold is added by the author.

Giving the Exchange
Jeff Musgrave

Cover design and page layout by Peter Crane

Greenville, South Carolina 29614
JourneyForth Books is a division of BJU Press.

Printed in the United States of America

ISBN 978-1-60682-185-5

15 14 13 12 11 10 9 8 7 6 5 4 3 2 1

DEDICATION

This book is dedicated to Dr. David Cummins. Though he has graduated to heaven, his influence in my life and ministry lingers heavily. I had the privilege of knowing him personally for only fifteen years. We began working together closely eleven years ago when Baptist World Mission asked me to train their deputizing missionaries. His insistence that I write my own soulwinning material gave birth to this book and now to the ministry of The Exchange. His kind, gentle, yet demanding confidence in me caused me to do far more with these resources than I ever would have without him.

CONTENTS

Teacher's lesson plans, tests, quizzes, and more are available to download at www.exchangemessage.org.

FOREWORD

Several years ago when I first began training the people of our church for evangelism, I would listen to recorded sessions taught by an experienced soulwinner and would teach exactly what he taught. When he told a soulwinning story, I would tell his story. God has accomplished something wonderful through these years of learning—I don't have to use someone else's stories anymore. This book has been several years in the making, and as I was finalizing it for publication, I was thrilled to relive the miraculous, life-transforming stories recorded here. It's worth the read just to see the power of the Savior displayed. My challenge for you is twofold. Give the gospel a chance!

- Thirty-Day Challenge—In the next thirty days give the gospel to someone or find someone with whom you can begin *The Exchange* Bible study.
- Ten-Year Challenge—Spend the next ten years accumulating your own stories of transformed lives. (Please email to tell us your first story at info@exchangemessage.org.)

Every Christian must be able to give a clear, compelling gospel presentation. Not only is this God's plan, but it's a command. Many believers "know" the gospel, but how many can articulate it clearly, thoroughly, and concisely? God's plan is to use the local church as the training arena to mobilize His children for soulwinning and discipleship. Therefore, it is necessary that every church have a systematic, reproducible training system. On the Job Training is a discipleship tool itself for the trainer/trainee. When the pastor's teaching in the classroom is reproduced by the trainer/trainee in someone's living room, the result is powerful!

The unique benefit of *Giving the Exchange* is its ability to be used in tandem with *The Exchange* Bible study. *Giving the Exchange* is actually a distillation of its corresponding four-lesson Bible study counterpart. While the twenty-minute presentation is thorough and compelling, the relationship-oriented Bible study affords four or more hours of exposure to the life-producing potential of the Word of God. The combined tools provide the resources to succeed in nearly every situation. Many of the stories in this book came about from situations in which the gospel was presented but the lost person just wasn't ready. So we offered a four-lesson Bible study. The rest is history.

Take the challenge but watch out! You will never be the same!

(Some of the names of people in the stories in this book have been changed.)

GIVING THE EXCHANGE OVERVIEW

CLASS DATE

________	Lesson 1	Introduction and Philosophy plus *Giving the Exchange* Gospel Presentation Demonstration (This is a three-hour lesson. There will be no On the Job Training this night.)
________	Lesson 2	What to Expect and Identifying Divine Appointments
________	Lesson 3	Making Friends Through Conversation
________	Lesson 4	Directing Conversation
________	Lesson 5	God Is Holy and Cannot Tolerate Our Sin
________	Lesson 6	God Is Just and Cannot Overlook Our Sin
________	Lesson 7	God Is Loving and Has Reached Out to Us
________	Lesson 8	God Is Gracious and Offers Salvation as a Gift
________	Lesson 9	Invitation
________	Lesson 10	Assimilation
________	Lesson 11	Practical Advice for Effective Soulwinners
________	Lesson 12	Verses Test, General Knowledge Review, and Q & A
________	Lesson 13	Turn in Oral Gospel Presentation One-Page Memory Sheet, Final Exam, and Testimonies

ON THE JOB TRAINING

The following list is provided for your trainer to check each time he or she leads your soulwinning team. Reading it each week will remind you what to pray for, aim at, and expect as you visit together.

TRAINER'S CHECK LIST

In the car

- ☐ Ask each team member to pray at the beginning of each On the Job Training excursion.
- ☐ Depend on Christ for boldness through the Holy Spirit. This will help instill boldness in your trainees.
- ☐ Take charge of where to go.
- ☐ Assign each team member his or her part in the visit.
- ☐ Plan when to "toss" the presentation to the trainee after Lesson 5.
- ☐ Anticipate God's divine appointments.
- ☐ Keep moving; find souls; use all the time you have.

- ☐ Use extra time in the car to practice the *Giving the Exchange* Gospel Presentation.
- ☐ Ensure spiritual conversation in the car.
- ☐ Lead a debriefing discussion that will assist in filling out the On the Job Training Debriefing Chart.
- ☐ Lead in prayer when you get back to church.

In the home

- ☐ Determine to get into homes.
- ☐ Ask, "May we come in?"
- ☐ Turn the conversation to the theme of themes and invite your new friend to "come and see the Lord."
- ☐ Use the *Giving the Exchange* Gospel Presentation.
- ☐ Use the religious questionnaire when your visits do not present an opportunity to witness.
- ☐ If you are not in a gospel presentation by 8:30, return to church.

In the trainee's life

- ☐ Endeavor to give the trainee experience.
- ☐ Don't let a week go by without the trainee hearing or saying the presentation in person. (If necessary, go to a church member who will listen or practice the presentation with your team.)
- ☐ Remember that "soulwinning is better caught than taught."
- ☐ Keep momentum going throughout the entire course, especially through the middle plateau. (Check to see if your trainee is caught up on all work and understands everything thus far.)
- ☐ *Philippians 1:6 —Being confident of this very thing, that he which hath begun a good work in you will perform it until the day of Jesus Christ.*

SECTION 1

RELATIONAL PHILOSOPHY

LESSON 1

ASSIGNMENT SHEET

- ☐ Read the Information Sheet and Lesson 1, "Introduction and Philosophy."
- ☐ Turn in Commitment Card.
- ☐ Read chapters 1–3 from *Just What the Doctor Ordered.*
- ☐ Pray about which two prayer partners you should ask.
- ☐ Watch the *Giving the Exchange* Gospel Presentation video at www.exchangemessage.org.
- ☐ Memorize Psalm 66:5*a*, 16*b* and 1 John 5:13.
- ☐ Memorize Lesson 1 Memory Sheet.
- ☐ Say Lesson 1 Memory Sheet out loud from memory in front of a mirror.
- ☐ Say Lesson 1 Memory Sheet to someone before class.
  Have him check the points you remember, listening for accuracy.
- ☐ Hand out five gospel tracts.
- ☐ Pray for the lost and for God's power on your life.

LESSON 1

ONE-PAGE **MEMORY SHEET**

"Come and see the works of God. . . . I will declare what he hath done for my soul." (Psalm 66:5a, 16b)

☐ **CONVERSATION**
I must turn the conversation to the theme of themes.

☐ **INTRODUCTION**
I must introduce the sinner to the Savior.

☐ ① **God Is Holy** and cannot tolerate our sin.

☐ ② **God Is Just** and cannot overlook our sin.

☐ ③ **God Is Loving** and has reached out to us.

☐ He has provided a way for us to be close to Him that satisfies His holy/just nature (John 3:16).

☐ ④ **God Is Gracious** and offers salvation as a gift.

☐ **INVITATION**
I must offer the inquirer the gift of eternal life.

☐ **ASSIMILATION**
I must call the disciple to the life of Christ.

LESSON 1

INTRODUCTION AND PHILOSOPHY

I. Inviting men to "come and see" Jesus

A. Christ's pattern—John 1

1. Jesus demonstrates.

When John's disciples asked Jesus where He was staying, He responded, "**Come and see**. They came and saw where he dwelt, and abode with him that day: for it was about the tenth hour" (John 1:39). Jesus didn't point the way. He walked beside them and showed them the way. This is relational!

2. Philip follows.

Philip's declaration: *John 1:45—Philip findeth Nathanael, and saith unto him, We have found him, of whom Moses in the law, and the prophets, did write, Jesus of Nazareth, the son of Joseph.*

Philip's invitation: *John 1:46—And Nathanael said unto him, Can there any good thing come out of Nazareth? Philip saith unto him,* ***Come and see****.*

Philip wasn't offended that Nathanael had insulted Philip's attempt to tell him about Jesus. He simply invited Nathanael to come and meet Jesus for himself. "If you know Him like I know Him, you'll love Him too."

Philip didn't try to convince him that Jesus was really born in Bethlehem or use apologetics to prove that He was the Messiah. He merely introduced him to Jesus and let Jesus convince him. The Holy Spirit is in the world today convincing men of sin, righteousness, and judgment. Our job is to introduce the sinner to the Savior. It is the Holy Spirit's job to do the convincing.

3. What does Jesus invite us to do? **Follow**.

John 1:43—The day following Jesus would go forth into Galilee, and findeth Philip, and saith unto him, ***Follow me****.*

John 21:19—This spake he, signifying by what death he should glorify God. And when he had spoken this, he saith unto him, ***Follow me****.*

Matthew 4:19—And he saith unto them, ***Follow me****, and I will make you fishers of men.*

Are you willing to follow Jesus and let Him make you a fisher of men?

The more intimately we **know** Jesus, the more effectively we will be able to **show** Him to the lost.

Acts 4:13—Now when they saw the boldness of Peter and John, and perceived that they were unlearned and ignorant men, they marvelled; and they took knowledge of them, that they had been with Jesus.

Knowing God intimately is one of the major themes of *Living the Exchange: A Disciple's Bible Study.*

B. Christ's parable—(go, find, and invite) Matthew 22:1–14

1. The invitations of the past—Matthew 22:2–7

These verses summarize all the invitations God gave to His people through the years only to be rejected.

2. The invitations of the end times/our times—Matthew 22:8–9

Then saith he to his servants, The wedding is ready, but they which were bidden were not worthy. ***Go*** *ye therefore into the highways, and as many as ye shall* ***find****, bid [****invite****] to the marriage.*

Our role in soulwinning is very simple. We are to **go** out, **find** men, and then **invite** them to "come and see" Jesus!

3. The instructions to the soulwinner—Matthew 22:10

a. We must **take steps** to obey/**go**—"so those servants **went**."

b. We must **find men**—"and gathered together all **as many as they found**."

1) Who? Whomever we find whether good or bad

2) Where? Wherever men might be found

c. We must **invite them**/gather them together—"**gathered together** all as many as they found, both bad and good: and the wedding was furnished with guests."

All they could do was invite. It is clear that many refused (note the context), but they invited enough that the wedding was furnished with guests! Are you going, finding, and inviting those around you? Is the "wedding" furnished with guests at your church?

We often prejudge people before we decide to witness to them based on how we think they will respond. Notice they invited "as many as they found, both bad and good."

II. God's church planting/growth model in Acts 11:20–26

The church will never be built without God's hand of blessing.

Acts 11:21—And the hand of the Lord was with them: and a great number believed, and turned unto the Lord.

A. Divine Appointment Concept

1. God is the Lord of the harvest. He sends us forth as reapers into His harvest. If we are to see souls saved for His glory, we must depend on Him to lead us to those He has prepared. See Matthew 9:36–38.

2. A divine appointment occurs when God sends us to someone in whose heart He is already working.

He is always at work around us. When we see His hand working in the lives around us, that is God inviting us to join Him in His work. See John 5:17–20.

3. Divine appointments emanate from a divine agenda.

   Luke 19:10—For the Son of man is come ***to seek and to save that which was lost.***

4. We can approach evangelism as a great treasure hunt rather than a sales event in which we are trying to convince someone to buy our religion. We may be tempted to use mental gymnastics to convince someone that their "facts" and worldview are wrong and ours are right. Our real job is to use our days looking for people in whom God is working and join Him by befriending them and showing them Who He really is.

GOD'S CHURCH PLANTING/GROWTH MODEL

(Each soul won and called to the life of Christ is a microcosm of planting a church.)

Conversation	λαλεω	"Spake"—Acts 11:20
Evangelization (introduction and invitation)	ευαγγελιζω	"Preaching"—Acts 11:20
Assimilation	παρακαλεω	"Exhorted"—Acts 11:23
Indoctrination (regular church involvement)	διδασκω	"Taught"—Acts 11:26

B. Relational Bridge Building

Four words are used to describe the communication involved in the first church plant in heathen territory. The first word is *conversation* and the second is *preaching*, or *evangelism*. The two words in *Giving the Exchange* that correspond to these words are *Conversation* and *Introduction*. A friendly, compelling conversation builds a bridge with the friend to whom we are talking in order to get an opportunity to introduce him to Jesus.

1. Conversation to introduction

   a. If someone asked you how to get to heaven, would you be willing to tell him? Would you know enough of the gospel to explain it to him? No doubt the answer to both of these questions is an unreserved yes. Our problem is not that we don't want to "preach." Our problem is not that we don't know what to say. Our problem is finding opportunities to give the gospel.

   "Soul-winners are not soul-winners because of **what** they know, but because of **the Person** they know, how well they know Him and how much they long for others to know Him."

   Dawson Trotman, *Born to Reproduce* (Colorado Springs: NavPress, no date), 34.

   b. **If we don't learn the art of making friends through compelling conversations, we will find very few opportunities to give the gospel.** Notice that in Antioch the early disciples turned their conversations into preaching opportunities. How many preaching opportunities do you get each day? How many conversations do you have each day? We must learn to turn our daily conversations into opportunities to introduce the people we meet to Jesus.

Clay Henry Trumbull's life resolve

As a young professional, Clay Trumbull worked as an office clerk and lived in a boarding house. One day a letter arrived from a friend back home. He went to a small map closet at work where he could be alone while he read the letter. It clearly told him how to be saved and made a personal appeal to receive Christ. He knelt on the floor of that closet and readily prayed the sinner's prayer. The next day on the way to work he took the opportunity to introduce a co-worker to his newfound joy and urged him to make the same decision.

The man's response burned another decision deep into Trumbull's heart. With shame and conviction his friend answered, "I've been a Christian since childhood, and never said a word that caused you to suspect it. I see now that you would have no doubt received Christ if I had but opened my mouth." That day Clay Trumbull made the following resolve which he kept the rest of his life:

> **"Whenever I am in such intimacy with a soul as to be justified in choosing my subject of conversation, the theme of themes shall have prominence between us, so that I may learn of his need, and if possible, meet it."**

Charles Gallaudet Trumbull, *Taking Men Alive* (NewYork: Fleming H. Revell Company, 1938), 65–69.

ANALYSIS

- In what way does this resolve guard against haphazard or discourteous efforts?
- In what circumstances does this resolve call for boldness?
- Why should each Christian make this same resolve?
- What is this resolve's definite and declared purpose?

Here is Trumbull's resolve in simpler language:

> **"I resolve to direct every conversation I possibly can to the theme of themes, learn of that soul's need, and if possible meet it."**

- Will you make this your life resolve?
- In what ways do you think it will change your life?

The next two actions, assimilation and indoctrination, are equally interrelated. Discipleship is a man-to-man relationship that builds a man-to-God relationship. **If we don't learn the relational aspect of discipleship in order to assimilate our new believers into our church families, very few converts will become fruitful believers.**

2. Assimilation to indoctrination

   a. We are called to indoctrinate our disciples by "teaching them to observe" everything Jesus has taught us. Most of our churches are good at teaching, but we are not very good at getting our new believers into church. The verb *exhorted*/παρακαλεω means "to call along side." The word *assimilate* means "to incorporate" or "to make a part of." God has called and equipped us to help new believers become a part of us. We must befriend them and do whatever is necessary to facilitate this process.

ILLUSTRATION

Imagine a mother telling her newborn, "Breakfast is at 8:00 a.m. Be there!" If the baby didn't come, would she say, "I guess he wasn't really born"? No! She takes breakfast to the baby. How long does she do this? **As long as it takes**.

I have found that many of us make this same assumption about our converts when they don't come to church after their conversion—"I guess he wasn't really born again." Maybe the problem is how we are caring for them.

Or can you imagine a mother allowing someone else to raise her baby? No! Except in extreme circumstances she would never allow this to happen. Why? Because that's her baby! The child belongs to her! May God give us this attitude toward our *spiritual babies*. "He belongs to me, and I am responsible for him."

b. Only when we befriend our new believers personally and facilitate functional relationships with other believers in our church will we have the ability to see them mature and be able to teach others also.

III. Introduction to *Giving the Exchange*

Giving the Exchange is thorough and theocentric, yet easy to memorize. It will equip you with all the necessary tools so that you can be used by the Holy Spirit as He draws men and women to Jesus. This is not about a plan of salvation but a Person of salvation. It introduces a new friend to the God of the Bible, and it invites him to see God as a person Who has specific characteristics and to see how those characteristics relate to him.

A. **Conversation**—We usually need to pave the way to introduce Jesus to a friend through a brief conversation that draws his heart to ours and turns his heart and mind to the gospel.

Resolve—I must turn the conversation to the theme of themes.

B. **Introduction**—Before we can expect a soul to make the decision to begin a relationship with God, it is imperative to introduce God as a person Who is knowable and has definable attributes.

Resolve—I must introduce the sinner to the Savior.

1. The Bible teaches us that the Holy Spirit came to convince the world of the truth about sin, righteousness, and judgment.

   John 16:8—And when he is come, he will reprove the world of sin, and of righteousness, and of judgment.

2. The apostles preached these same three themes.

   Acts 24:25—And as he reasoned of righteousness, temperance, and judgment to come, Felix trembled, and answered, Go thy way for this time; when I have a convenient season, I will call for thee.

   Paul declared the truth about God, and the Holy Spirit convinced Felix of its truth. He didn't use apologetics or intellectual prowess. He declared simple truths to Felix and expected the Holy Spirit to convince him. By the fact that Felix trembled, it is clear that he felt the need of his heart even though he did not make a decision.

3. *Giving the Exchange* emphasizes a clear, compelling presentation of the gospel as opposed to an apologetic approach. It is aimed at the heart rather than the mind. While not bypassing the mind, we recognize the need to go deeper into our friend's soul. We must rely on the power of the gospel to

convince the sinner of His need and draw him to the Savior.

*Romans 1:16—For I [Paul] am not ashamed of the **gospel of Christ**: for it is the **power of God unto salvation** to every one that believeth.*

*John 12:32—And I [Jesus], if I be lifted up from the earth, **will draw all men unto me**.*

Rather than start with the premise that man has a problem and needs God, ***Giving the Exchange*** **begins with a simple introduction to God as a person and how He relates to man**. It is designed to show a sinner that

- God is holy and cannot tolerate our sin. (Sin)
- God is just and cannot overlook our sin. (Judgment)
- God is loving and has reached out to us. He has provided a way for us to be close to Him. (Righteousness provided)
- God is gracious and offers salvation as a gift. (Righteousness obtained)

C. **Invitation**—*Giving the Exchange* will guide you to draw your friend to a decision in a direct, yet smooth, sequence that allows the Holy Spirit to convert a sinner without man's manipulation.

Resolve—I must offer the inquirer the gift of eternal life.

D. **Assimilation**—Jesus said in John 15:16, "I have chosen you . . . that ye should go and bring forth fruit, and that **your fruit should remain**." The context of this verse indicates that we are to teach our "fruit" how to abide in Christ. This portion of the presentation is only an introduction to his newly obtained riches in Christ and is designed to encourage the new believer to plumb the depths of his inheritance by committing to study *Living the Exchange*.

Resolve—I must call the disciple to the life of Christ.

IV. The priorities of *Giving the Exchange*

A. **To know Christ intimately and to show Him effectively** by allowing Him to use us in His ministry of transforming lives

B. **To train men and women to be diligent, effective laborers** in the Master's plenteous harvest fields in both evangelism and discipleship

C. **To equip men and women to train others**

V. Why's of *Giving the Exchange*

A. **The Command**—We are all commanded to make disciples and effectively assimilate them into a church home. Every believer is personally responsible to obey this command and will give an account to God for it. See 2 Corinthians 5:10–11.

Matthew 28:19–20—Go ye therefore, and teach all nations, baptizing them in the name of the Father, and of the Son, and of the Holy Ghost: teaching them to observe all things whatsoever I have commanded you: and, lo, I am with you alway, even unto the end of the world. Amen.

B. **The Church**—This Great Commission work is accomplished primarily through the local church. Every church has the responsibility to train its members in evangelism. That's how churches grow. God's plan is for the leaders of the church to train the members of the church to do kingdom work.

Ephesians 4:11–12—And he gave some, apostles; and some, prophets; and some, evangelists; and some, pastors and teachers; for the perfecting [equipping] of the saints, for [into] the work of the ministry, for the edifying of the body of Christ.

2 Timothy 2:2—And the things that thou hast heard of me among many witnesses, the same commit thou to faithful men, who shall be able to teach others also.

C. **The Approach**—On the Job Training

Evangelism is better caught than taught. I have never met anyone who became a soulwinner in a classroom. Ask any good soulwinner how he became one and he will more than likely tell you that his pastor, Sunday school teacher, or friend took him under his wing and showed him how. An evangelism program works only if the training is reproducible. What is taught in the classroom must be seen by a trainee during live soulwinning experiences.

1. Relationship of the Word and work

   a. Seeing the Word—Some people choose to believe the **words** of God and as a result see the **work** of God accomplished.

   Matthew 4:19—And he saith unto them, Follow me, and I will make you fishers of men.

   Romans 10:17—So then faith cometh by hearing, and hearing by the ***word*** *of God.*

   b. Seeing the work—Other people have to see the **works** of God before they believe the **Word** of God.

   John 10:37–38—If I do not the works of my Father, believe me not. But if I do, though ye ***believe not me, believe the works: that ye may know, and believe****, that the Father is in me, and I in him.*

   John 14:12—Verily, verily, I say unto you, ***He that believeth on me, the works that I do shall he do also****; and greater works than these shall he do; because I go unto my Father.*

2. Some Laws of Christian Dynamics

   a. *Inertia Principle*
   Getting started is the hardest part.
   All humans tend to return to inactivity.

   b. *Activity Principle*
   Desire is no substitute for activity.
   Activity is no substitute for productivity.
   We put our faith on display through grace-infused activity.

   c. *Discipline Principle*
   External discipline without a matching internal desire eventually fails.

   d. *Programs*
   Sermons speak for a day or so; programs speak every week for as long as they are used.

   e. *Personal Effort Principle*
   Programs don't work by themselves. They must be made to work by personal effort.

   f. *Pacesetter*
   People learn best by following the example of a pacesetter and forming a close relationship with him.

D. **Our Confidence**—God is in the soulwinning business, and He will give us souls.

Acts 11:21—And the hand of the Lord was with them: and a great number believed, and turned unto the Lord.

Psalm 126:5–6—They that sow in tears shall reap in joy. He that goeth forth and weepeth, bearing precious seed, shall doubtless come again with ***rejoicing, bringing*** *his sheaves with him.*

See the chart God's Plan to Preach the Gospel to Every Creature on page 16.

VI. The Exchange circle of ministry

The Exchange: *An Inquirer's Bible Study* is a four-lesson Bible study that deals with the same four attributes of God that are taught in *Giving the Exchange*. The vast majority of people who complete *The Exchange* Bible study are either saved during the process or come to assurance of their salvation.

Living the Exchange: *A Disciple's Bible Study* is a twelve-lesson Bible study that teaches the dynamics of the Christian life. It is written in the same interactive style found in *The Exchange* Bible study. Many who have completed this study have grown to new heights in their Christian life. The last lesson in *Living the Exchange* emphasizes the importance of ministry in the local church, especially evangelism.

Giving the Exchange: *A Course in Relational Evangelism and Discipleship* is designed to complete the circle of ministry by preparing the maturing Christian to be an effective disciple-maker himself.

VII. Relational evangelism and discipleship

A. Witness to those with whom you have existing relationships.

1. Andrew found his own brother Peter. See John 1:37–42.

2. Jesus found Philip. See John 1:43.

3. Philip found Nathanael. See John 1:45–46.

MARY ELLEN

Vann and Mary Ellen visited our church, and my wife and I were in their home the following Tuesday evening. Mary Ellen claimed to know the Lord but was so talkative it was hard to determine Vann's need. I asked him to lunch. Since he was retired and loved intellectual discussion, he readily agreed. During the meal I asked him to do a four-lesson Bible study about Who God is and how He relates to us. Anna and I began to go to their home every Tuesday evening, first for dinner and then for Bible study. Not only did both of them accept the Lord during those weeks, but we became very good friends. Little did we know that 289 days after Vann trusted Christ as his personal Savior, he would be in heaven.

Michael and Renee came to Vann's memorial service, which was held in our church. They had loved Vann and were touched by the confidence Mary Ellen displayed that Vann was in heaven. Mary Ellen asked them if they would like to do the Bible study that she and Vann had done and then invited Anna and me to join them. Michael and Renee both made their salvation sure during the Bible study and began attending church regularly with Mary Ellen.

Michael is a gregarious man and a runner. He asked his neighbor Jonathan to join him for a run and during the run invited him to do the Bible study. Michael asked our assistant pastor to do the Bible study with Jonathan and Monica, and they were both saved after lesson 3.

Two and a half years after Vann's death, Mary Ellen did the Bible study with Vann's daughter, and she was saved after lesson 4.

These stories are the natural result of caring relationships and bold witnesses.

What existing relationships should you utilize?

B. Make relationships for the purpose of witnessing (redemptive relationships).

1. Jesus healed a man at the pool of Bethesda and then purposely reunited with him later to help him with his spiritual needs. See John 5:1–14.

   The key is to recognize that God is always at work and invites us to join Him in that work by giving us a glimpse into what He is doing. We must develop an eye to see His hand and an ear to hear Him nudge us toward the people He wants us to reach. See John 5:17–21.

2. Matthew had a dinner for his unsaved friends so that he could introduce them to Jesus. See Luke 5:27–29.

   Some people are "connectors" who seem to make friends wherever they go. Though your personality may be different, you can practice being more friendly (Proverbs 18:24), and you can ask the Lord for ideas that will enable you to reach lost people by forming deepening relationships.

   - Have a block party.
   - Host a Christmas open house.
   - Host a ladies' tea.
   - Have a birthday party.
   - Join a sports team.
   - Run or walk with a neighbor.
   - Invite a neighbor or friend to dinner.
   - Get to know the parents of the teammates on your child's sports team.
   - Join the PTA or volunteer at school.
   - Volunteer at a hospital, pregnancy counseling center, the Red Cross, etc.

   What are some other places to look for new friends and build redemptive relationships?
   It is important not to let your life get so busy, even with church events, that you don't have time to meet new friends.

3. FIND FIVE—Always have five people for whom you are praying and trying to befriend. To borrow a term from social networking, you need to expand your "fan base."

   F—family and friends

   A—associates at work or play

   N—neighbors

   S—strangers God brings into your path

C. Form relationships with those to whom you witness.

Though Jesus had never met Nicodemus or the woman at the well (John 3–4), He dealt with them relationally and was able to uniquely touch each one, creating a deep, long-lasting relationship.

Discipleship is a man-to-man relationship that builds a man-to-God relationship. Discipleship begins with evangelism. Matthew 28:19 teaches that evangelism is disciple-making. **Everything changes when we begin evangelism with a discipleship mentality.**

VIII. The Vision

*Proverbs 29:18*a—***Where there is no vision, the people perish.***

This story is based on an old sermon illustration. Though fictitious, it has been repeated many times in real life.

JACK

Jack was on his way home for the first time in twenty-five years. He remembered the last day he had seen the old building. He was much younger then. He had grown up in that church. His best memories were of the missionaries that preached there. Jack could see Pastor Jenkins now, the pastor's eyes burning as missionary after missionary reminded the congregation of the call to reach the world. He remembered the teens in the youth group meeting each Sunday night before evening service to pray about missions. How Jack had longed to be old enough to be a part of their number. He wondered how many of those teens were still burdened for missions today. He should have kept in touch.

He remembered how fast that time had gone. He was just a child wishing he could be a part of the activity. Then he was in the midst of the activity, and the burden for reaching the world with the gospel message was so real it consumed his thinking. He remembered the missions conference when Pastor Jenkins hung the sign in the back of the auditorium, **"Where there is no vision, the people perish."** That was the week he finally surrendered to be a missionary. In the back of his mind he sensed that God had called him, but that Sunday he **knew** for the first time that God wanted **him** to be a missionary. Then he was off to Bible college with only brief visits home now and then. He remembered how feeble Pastor Jenkins looked at his commissioning service and wasn't surprised to learn of his home going while he was in language school.

Pastor Jenkins may have been feeble, but he was still sharp; and Jack remembered with a thankful heart how his pastor had stopped a line of questioning at his ordination council. Jack remembered wondering how he should answer the question on predestination. His thoughts whirled! It seemed that the question grew wings as one man after another added his spin on it. Pastor Jenkins had placed a reassuring hand on Jack's shoulder and said, "This question has been debated for decades, and we on the council can't even agree on the answer. I don't think it's appropriate to have this young missionary drawn into it. Jack, why don't you tell them about your burden for the Congo?"

Jack remembered that same hand—heavy, yet comforting on his shoulder as the deacons and Pastor Jenkins laid hands on him that next day and commissioned him to be their missionary. What a weight of responsibility and sense of confidence they laid on him that day. Then there was the memory of the people standing in front of that old vibrant country church waving goodbye; there was the last minute prayer with Pastor at the train station, and then he was gone.

That was twenty-five years ago. It had been hard not to be able to go home when his parents died suddenly in the accident, but they were buried in the churchyard by the time word got to him. Besides, the work was thriving and there was no one to take his place. He had received letters from the ladies' missionary society for some years, but they began to dwindle. It had been three years since he had heard anything.

As he rounded the corner he was devastated by what he saw. The building was faded, with white paint peeling from its warped siding. Some of the tall, narrow windows were broken and ugly. The grass was wild and unmowed. Even the hitching post was broken. Jack walked up the tilted stairs and peered in the window on the door. He was not surprised to find that it was unlocked. No one had ever locked the doors to this church. He could almost hear the voices of the congregation singing as he walked down the squeaky wood floor of the center aisle. Some of the hymnbooks were still in their racks, but the dust of disuse was thick. Jack was confused. How could this happen? He remembered such life in this room, and now it was as if he were walking in a mausoleum. He climbed up the creaking steps to the old ornate pulpit, ran his hands over its dusty top, and turned to look back at what used to be. Then he saw it! On the back wall, the sign that had been put up years ago in the height of zeal was sagging and broken. The part remaining on the wall spelled out what had happened to the life of this church:

". . . no vision, the people perish."

The word *vision* means "divine communication." Vision is larger than what we are doing and, in some cases, larger than what we are able to do. Vision encompasses the goals at which we are aiming. The word *perish* means "to let go, to neglect, or to loosen." Let God's inner voice stir you daily and plan to stay zealous in the ministry of reaching the lost. You have been given the ability. Determine to keep your vision clear so that you don't neglect those in need.

Jesus said, "And I will give unto thee the keys of the kingdom of heaven: and whatsoever thou shalt bind on earth shall be bound in heaven: and whatsoever thou shalt loose on earth shall be loosed in heaven" (Matthew 16:19).

- What vision God is giving you?
- How is God accomplishing this vision through you?
- What are the changes He is asking you to make?
- What changes are you willing to make right now?

GOD'S PLAN TO PREACH THE GOSPEL TO EVERY CREATURE

If you and I were both gifted evangelists and were able to lead **1,000** souls to the Lord every week, that would equal **104,000** souls in one year! If we were able to do that for sixteen years, we would be privileged to see **1,664,000** souls brought into the kingdom of God!

But if you and I each determined to ask God for just one soul every six months, then trained that one soul to do the same, and each of us continued that trend, this would be the result!

Years	Six month periods	Existing believers	New believers	Total believers
	1	2	2	4
1	2	4	4	8
	3	8	8	16
2	4	16	16	32
	5	32	32	64
3	6	64	64	128
	7	128	128	256
4	8	256	256	512
	9	512	512	1,024
5	10	1,024	1,024	2,048
	11	2,048	2,048	4,096
6	12	4,096	4,096	8,192
	13	8,192	8,192	16,384
7	14	16,384	16,384	32,768
	15	32,768	32,768	65,536
8	16	65,536	65,536	131,072
	17	131,072	131,072	262,144
9	18	262,144	262,144	524,288
	19	524,288	524,288	1,048,576
10	20	1,048,576	1,048,576	2,097,152
	21	2,097,152	2,097,152	4,194,304
11	22	4,194,304	4,194,304	8,388,608
	23	8,388,608	8,388,608	16,777,216
12	24	16,777,216	16,777,216	33,554,432
	25	33,554,432	33,554,432	67,108,864
13	26	67,108,864	67,108,864	134,217,728
	27	134,217,728	134,217,728	268,435,456
14	28	268,435,456	268,435,456	536,870,912
	29	536,870,912	536,870,912	1,073,741,824
15	30	1,073,741,824	1,073,741,824	2,147,483,648
	31	2,147,483,648	2,147,483,648	4,294,967,296
16	32	4,294,967,296	4,294,967,296	8,589,934,592

In sixteen years we could reach the world's population.
I'll start now. Will you?

LESSON 2

ASSIGNMENT SHEET

- ☐ Ask two people to be your prayer partners while you go through *Giving the Exchange.*
- ☐ Turn in your Prayer Partner Cards to your leader.
- ☐ Pray with your prayer partners.
- ☐ Read Lesson 2, "What to Expect and Identifying Divine Appointments."
- ☐ Read chapters 4–6 from *Just What the Doctor Ordered.*
- ☐ Memorize Titus 3:5 and Habakkuk 1:13*a.*
- ☐ Memorize Lesson 2 Memory Sheet.
- ☐ Say Lesson 2 Memory Sheet out loud from memory in front of a mirror.
- ☐ Say Lesson 2 Memory Sheet to someone before class.
  Have him check the points you remember, listening for accuracy.
- ☐ Hand out five gospel tracts.
- ☐ Pray for the lost and for God's power on your life.
- ☐ Make a Find Five List and formulate a plan with your trainer to reach the people on it.

LESSON 2

ONE-PAGE **MEMORY SHEET**

"Come and see the works of God. . . . I will declare what he hath done for my soul." (Psalm 66:5a, 16b)

☐ CONVERSATION

I must turn the conversation to the theme of themes.

- ☐ ① **Making Conversation**
- ☐ ② **Directing Conversation**
- ☐ "How would you describe your relationship with God?"
- ☐ "What do you think it takes to have a relationship with God and live with Him forever in heaven?"
- ☐ Personal Testimony—He has changed my life.
- ☐ "Are you 100% sure that all your sins are forgiven and you will go to heaven?"
- ☐ 1 John 5:13 or Titus 3:5
- ☐ "May I show you from the Bible how to have a relationship with God?"

☐ INTRODUCTION

I must introduce the sinner to the Savior.

- ☐ ① **God Is Holy** and cannot tolerate our sin.
- ☐ ② **God Is Just** and cannot overlook our sin.
- ☐ ③ **God Is Loving** and has reached out to us.
- ☐ He has provided a way for us to be close to Him that satisfies His holy/just nature (John 3:16).
- ☐ ④ **God Is Gracious** and offers salvation as a gift.

☐ INVITATION

I must offer the inquirer the gift of eternal life.

☐ ASSIMILATION

I must call the disciple to the life of Christ.

LESSON 2

WHAT TO EXPECT AND IDENTIFYING DIVINE APPOINTMENTS

I. Requirements for *Giving the Exchange*

A. You must have assurance of your salvation before you can lead others to Christ.

B. You must be a vessel of honor.

1. Purity of the vessel: *2 Timothy 2:21—If a man therefore purge himself from these, he shall be a vessel unto honour, sanctified, and meet for the master's use, and prepared unto every good work.*

2. Purging of the flesh: *2 Timothy 2:22–23—Flee also youthful lusts: but follow righteousness, faith, charity, peace, with them that call on the Lord out of a pure heart. But foolish and unlearned questions avoid, knowing that they do gender strifes.*

3. Preparation of the soul: *2 Timothy 2:24—And the servant of the Lord must not strive; but be gentle unto all men, apt to teach, patient.*

4. Passion of a lifetime: *2 Timothy 2:25–26—In meekness instructing those that oppose themselves; if God peradventure will give them repentance to the acknowledging of the truth; and that they may recover themselves out of the snare of the devil, who are* ***taken captive*** *by him at his will.*

   Taken captive is from the same Greek word found in Luke 5:10*b*. "Fear not; from henceforth thou shalt ***catch*** [catch alive] men." If we don't capture men for Christ, they will remain enslaved in Satan's cruel clutches for all eternity.

C. You must be filled with the Spirit of God.

1. *Luke 24:49—And, behold, I send the promise of my Father upon you: but tarry ye in the city of Jerusalem, until ye be endued with power from on high.*

   We no longer need to **wait** for the promise, but we do need to live in the power of the Lord by faith and go out anticipating His blessings because of it.

2. *1 Corinthians 2:4—And my speech and my preaching was not with enticing words of man's wisdom, but in* ***demonstration*** *of the Spirit and of power.*

Paul gives a beautiful description of Spirit-filled evangelism and discipleship in 1 Thessalonians 1:9–2:12.

D. You must make a commitment to do this ministry in the power of the Holy Spirit. We demonstrate our dependence on Him through the following:

1. Prayer—You will be asked to enlist two prayer partners and pray once a week.
2. Perseverance—If God is really calling you to this ministry, He will help you complete all the memory work and assignments.
3. Faithfulness—Expect God to create divine appointments for you during On the Job Training. Knowing you will be used by Him will instill faithfulness.

E. You must be willing to let the Lord empower you to become an effective mouthpiece for Deity. We will discuss this more in the next lesson.

II. What to expect from being involved in *Giving the Exchange*

A. You will see God work and the Devil attack. Be prepared for both.

B. You are now part of a team. You will probably develop a growing relationship with your partners as you assault the gates of hell together.

1. Let the trainer lead you and your discussions in the car.
2. Watch as he teaches by example to depend on the Lord to get you into homes and open doors to present the gospel.
3. Your trainer should encourage you to say the *Giving the Exchange* One-Page Memory Sheet and ask you about your homework. Always be transparent, even if you are struggling.

C. *Giving the Exchange* is a demanding class. The assignments are proportioned to maximize learning. Please do your homework every week so that you don't fall behind.

D. The class structure will be similar each week. (You will need to be on time to get everything done.)

1. Quiz over memory work and assignment collection
2. Brief testimonies about relational evangelism opportunities
3. Demonstration of the gospel presentation segment
(You will be requested to write down questions or comments while you are observing.)
4. Discussion of the how's and why's of the demonstration
5. Gospel presentation practice

E. On the Job Training is the heart of this course. You will put into practice what you learn in class. You must complete a minimum of ten hours to receive your certificate of completion.

When you have completed the course, you will, Lord willing, be confident that God can use you to lead lost souls to Him.

III. Looking for divine appointments

A. Definition—A divine appointment is when God providentially empowers you to touch a life in which He is already working.

1. There are two key elements of a divine appointment—providence and evidence.
2. Divine appointments emanate from a divine agenda.
3. You know you're in a divine appointment when
   - you enter a situation and it is obvious that God has been at work before you got there.
   - the person to whom you are talking tells you that someone else has been talking to him about the Lord.
   - you see obvious interest or conviction.
   - the Lord leads you to say something you normally don't say.
   - a lost person approaches a Christian out of the blue.
   - the timing of the events is obviously from God.
   - the person to whom you are talking is dealing with a traumatic event that has pointed him to his inner needs.
   - a visitor comes to your church without a human invitation.
   - someone brings up the Bible, religion, God, or spiritual things in a normal conversation.

B. Modern-day examples of divine appointments

1. SHERRY

I was sitting next to a man on an airplane who was showing a picture he was drawing to a little girl a couple of aisles away. When I asked him if they were traveling together, I found out that she was his daughter, and I volunteered to trade places with her. I ended up sitting next to a woman named Sherry, who was so shy she had a hard time looking at me while she was talking. After getting to know her, I directed the conversation to spiritual things and asked her about her relationship with God. She was visibly moved and said, "My daughter has been talking to me about this."

I told her I thought God had moved me to sit next to her and asked her if she would let me show her from the Bible how to have a relationship with God. She said yes and listened intently but was too shy to trust Christ on the plane. I urged her to make the decision before the day was over, gave her a "Do You Know God Personally?" tract, and wrote my address on it, asking her to let me know when she made the decision. (These tracts are available at www.exchangemessage.org.)

It was nearly two months later when I received this letter from her:

Jeff Musgrave

I don't know if you remember me, but I have something to tell you. You sat next to me on an airplane going from Indianapolis to St. Louis. You had to change seats with a little girl who was sitting next to me. Her father was drawing a dragon, I think. Anyway, you asked if it was OK if you talked to me about God. I guess you thought at first I wasn't interested because of the expression on my face. But the expression had a reason behind it, which at the time I didn't want any one to know about. My reaction was, "Well God, you got me 35,000 feet in the air, and now I can't run." You told me you thought God put you there to talk to me. Well He did!

Before I went on my trip I had been seeing several doctors and surgeons and had just found out that I had inflammatory breast cancer. It is a cancer that only five percent of women in the world get. And I knew when I was going back home I would be going through six to twelve months of chemotherapy and having my breasts removed, not to mention my long hair.

I told my daughter when I got home what happened on the airplane when you talked to me, and she began to cry. She said everything was going to be OK and that I really didn't know how many people are praying for me. She said that everyone from her church [was also praying] and I guess you now know why I had that OH MY! expression on my face. You are a wonderful person. I understand what you were telling me—believe me!

Merry Christmas to you and your family, and thank you

God Bless You
Sherry

2. JEWISH WOMAN

We were conducting an evangelism seminar at our church in Colorado. During one of the scheduled On the Job Training times, one of the pastors attending the seminar knocked on the door of a Jewish woman. She was very interested, and the pastor began to share the gospel with her. It was a beautiful Colorado evening, and all the time they were talking on the woman's front porch they could hear someone shoveling gravel just around the corner of the house. They were talking about God's justice when the woman's husband stepped around the corner with the shovel still in his hand and said to her, "I want these people off my porch now!"

The pastor told us later that he had just learned about divine appointments and was sure that if God wanted him to finish the presentation the Lord would provide a way. He calmly turned to the woman and asked if she wanted them to leave. She looked at her husband and replied, "I want to hear what they have to say."

He turned in a huff, and she asked the pastor to continue. That's a divine appointment.

3. SARAH

Andy was looking for someone with whom to start a four-lesson Bible study when he met a young woman who had been in a serious auto accident. She was recovering from her injuries and was still shaken from the experience. He told her he felt it was no accident that they had met and made the statement, "In times like this, you need the Lord."

Her response indicated that she agreed wholeheartedly but that she did not feel very close to Him. Andy asked if she would like to spend some time getting to know God better by doing *The Exchange* Bible study with him and his wife, Jenny. They started right away and were only two weeks into the lesson when Sarah trusted Christ as her Savior.

4. YOUNG COUPLE

   While hosting another evangelism seminar in our church, I was leading a team during the first On the Job Training night. While talking to the pastor and our other partner, I missed the exit I was supposed to take and had to drive several more miles out of the way. While I was thinking about what I would do, I noticed that I was on empty and would have to stop to get gas before we proceeded. I was disappointed with wasting so much time, and while I was filling the car, I took out our visitation notebook to find a closer visit. I had five visits in my book, and the "best" ones on the top were all far from where we were. The one on the bottom of the stack, which was a backup just in case no one else was home, was only a few blocks away.

   I decided we would go there since we had already wasted so much time. It was in an apartment complex, and a young man opened the door, stepped out, and pulled the door shut, holding the doorknob in both hands behind him. His body language was not very promising, to say the least. I introduced myself and my two teammates and said, "Sue from our church called and talked to Chris. Chris said she was interested in some information about our church, and Sue asked us to bring it by. May we come in?"

   He opened the door and called over his shoulder, "There are some people here from the church. Do you want to talk to them?"

   She said yes and the apartment we stepped into revealed a very strange scene. A couch loaded with clean, unfolded laundry and a coffee table were the only pieces of furniture in a fairly spacious living room. A young woman and a middle-aged woman were sitting on the floor counting stacks of money. I could see chairs around the kitchen table, asked if we could use them, and got everyone seated before we began the conversation in earnest. I have to admit my bungling didn't stop with the empty gas tank. When I began to turn the conversation to spiritual things, the young woman said, "We've been studying the Bible every night. We want to know how to live forever."

   I was so surprised and thrilled that I went right into the gospel without gathering the information I usually do. I had to stop in the middle of the presentation and go back to ask some diagnostic questions. Upon doing so, I discovered that the older woman already knew the Lord. I also found out she was the younger woman's mother and that the younger woman's identical twin had recently been killed in an auto accident. They had donated her organs for transplants, and the money on the floor was from selling T-shirts to raise money for a local donation program. Both the young woman and the young man were saved that night. It was clear that despite my bungling, God wanted us in that apartment that night.

C. Biblical examples of divine appointments

1. *Acts 18:10*b—*I have much people in this city.*

   When the Lord made this statement in a night vision to Paul, he was in Corinth before the church there had been started. It was just after the Jews in Corinth had rejected the gospel; and as far as we know, there were no other Christians in the city. Who was God referring to? He was telling Paul about the souls He was preparing to receive the gospel. God was letting Paul know there were divine appointments awaiting him in Corinth. See Acts 18:9–11.

2. *Luke 5:10*b—*From henceforth thou shalt catch men.*

   Jesus not only knew the disciples would see many come to Him but promised to prepare the way for them.

3. *2 Timothy 2:25–26—In meekness instructing those that oppose themselves; if God peradventure will give them repentance to the acknowledging of the truth.*

   God brings men to repentance; that's not our job. Even now He is preparing souls to whom He wants us to speak.

4. *John 16:8—And when he [the Holy Spirit] is come, he will reprove [convince] the world of sin, and of righteousness, and of judgment.*

   The Comforter has come! He is doing His work of convincing. Our job is not to convince men but to find the ones He is convincing and invite then to "come and see" Jesus.

5. *Genesis 24:27*b*—I being in the way, the Lord led me.*

   Abraham's servant was commissioned to find a bride for his master's son. Through prayer and providence God clearly led him to Rebekah. Upon telling her family of his purpose, she agreed to leave with him the very next day. He brought her to Isaac, knowing she was the woman God had prepared for him. Through prayer and providence the Holy Spirit will lead us to those He is preparing to come to the Savior, but we have to be "in the way."

6. *Acts 8:29–40—Then the Spirit said unto Philip, Go near, and join thyself to this chariot.*

   Philip and the Ethiopian is a marvelous story of the Holy Spirit's preparation of a sinner and His prompting of a soulwinner. Though the Ethiopian had been in Jerusalem and had a copy of Scripture, he still needed a soulwinner. Philip was sent by the Lord away from a revival to a desert for no apparent reason, yet he obeyed. It was not until he was prompted by the Holy Spirit to join the traveling Ethiopian that he could observe he was reading a passage in the Scripture that foretold in detail the crucifixion of Christ. He had indeed been prepared to hear the gospel message, and the prepared sinner was quick to receive the Lord Jesus as soon as he had heard of Jesus' finished work. The Holy Spirit is still preparing sinners and prompting soulwinners. May we have ears that hear and feet that obey!

7. *Acts 24:24*b*—He [Felix] sent for Paul, and heard him concerning the faith in Christ.*

   When Paul preached sin, righteousness, and judgment, Felix trembled. The Holy Spirit was doing His work in Felix's heart, though he procrastinated making a decision.

D. Two ways to find divine appointments

1. **Take the opportunity**—Carpe diem (seize the day).

   Be soul conscious. Always live conscious of the souls around you and look for needs that God might use you to meet. Look for the opportunities that God sends your way.

   a. When Nicodemus came to Jesus by night, Jesus was quick to see that he was open to the truth and presented it to him in a captivating, compelling way. As far as we know, he did not make a decision until after the crucifixion, but it is clear this conversation with the Master was a divine appointment.

   b. BARBARA
   I was sitting in my office when Barbara, a county inspector, came to our church to look at some construction we were doing. There was no foreman on the job, so I met her in the parking lot and escorted her to the building she was to inspect. As we were walking, she gestured to the main

building and said, "So this is a Baptist church, huh?"

It was as if she were tossing me a softball to see how far I could hit it. She was fruit ready to be plucked. After giving her the gospel, she exclaimed, "I just did that last night, while reading my Bible."

Barbara became a faithful member of our church, and when she was baptized, she stood in the baptistery and introduced herself as if in an AA meeting, "Hello, I'm Barbara, and I'm a sinner."

2. **Make the opportunity.**

   a. Some might say, "I don't schedule soulwinning. I just live in soul consciousness." But if they let weeks go by without witnessing to anyone, they are disobedient.

   b. If there are no obvious soulwinning opportunities, do right anyway!

   PHIL

   Phil had been told that if he lived a good Christian life, people would notice something different about him and ask him about it. When they asked, he would have an open door to witness. To his credit, he wasn't very satisfied with the results, so he approached me to see what I thought. "I don't get very many people who ask me about being a Christian. Would it be okay if I asked them first?"

   c. Jesus gave a parable that clearly identifies our responsibility in soulwinning.

   *Matthew 22:9—**Go** ye therefore into the highways, and as many as ye shall **find**, bid [**invite**] to the marriage.*

E. God can work anytime.

1. In Luke 5 Peter had been fishing all night. Having caught nothing, he had quit and was cleaning his nets the next morning when Jesus asked him to take Him fishing. Peter knew it was a bad time to fish, but at Jesus' request he obeyed. Jesus knew where the fish were and instructed the fisherman where to lower his nets. They caught more fish than two boats could hold, and Peter fell down at Jesus' feet and worshiped him as Lord.

   Jesus promised us in Luke 5:10 that we will catch men when we **go fishing with Him**. He still knows where the fish are, but we have to "launch out into the deep" before He will show us where to fish.

2. John 4 shows **Jesus making an opportunity**. He said He "must needs go through Samaria." Upon finding the women at the well, He asked, "Give me to drink," beginning a conversation that ended with her being saved and leading many in Samaria to "come, see" Jesus for themselves.

   Sometimes the opportunities to invite people to "come and see" Jesus are not as obvious as others, but we are still commanded to do it. So, whether we **take an opportunity** or **make an opportunity**, we are still dependent on the Lord for leadership and guidance.

F. The biblical pattern of finding divine appointments

1. Diligently sow and reap

   Mark 4:3—Hearken; Behold, there went out a sower to sow.

Mark 4:29—But when the fruit is brought forth, immediately he putteth in the sickle, because the harvest is come.

2. Constantly look to the fields

   a. **What Jesus saw:** *John 4:35—Say not ye, There are yet four months, and then cometh harvest? behold, I say unto you, Lift up your eyes, and look on the fields; for they are white already to harvest.*

      The disciples were looking for a future harvest. Jesus saw a harvest that was ripe and ready to be picked. **We need these words today as much as the disciples did.** Many of us plan to win souls and would like to see people saved, but rarely do. If this sounds like you, you need to

      1) Lift up your eyes. (You may have to get your eyes off yourself first.)

      2) Look unto the fields.

      3) Keep looking until you find.

         KEITH

         Sometimes we argue with God about the lack of ready fruit. One summer my wife spent ten days on an evangelistic campaign in the Philippines. She worked tirelessly and personally talked to hundreds of people, watching the majority of them trust Christ. During the same time, I started *The Exchange* Bible study with a couple who visited our church. Five weeks later, the woman got assurance of her salvation and the man got saved. Though the fields vary in productivity, there is fruit everywhere; and God has commanded us to keep looking to the fields. He knows we will find fruit if we don't faint.

   b. **What Jesus knew:** *Matthew 9:35–36 —And Jesus went about all the cities and villages,* ***teaching*** *in their synagogues, and* ***preaching*** *the gospel of the kingdom, and healing every sickness and every disease among the people. But when he saw the multitudes, he was moved with compassion on them, because they fainted, and were scattered abroad, as sheep having no shepherd.*

      1) "Fainted"—something going wrong?

      2) "Scattered"—loneliness?

      3) "Having no shepherd"—needing direction?

      Jesus "was moved with compassion." Jesus is still moved with compassion for people in need. His Spirit lives in you and will move you to compassion if you will slow down and look for needs.

      Questions you can ask to find out what God is doing in a person's life

      - How can I pray for you?
      - Do you want to talk about it?
      - What do you see as the greatest challenge in your life?
      - What is the most significant thing that is happening in your life right now?
      - What do you think God is trying to do in your life?

3. Consistently expect to harvest (practice the promises)

   Matthew 9:37–38—Then saith he unto his disciples, ***The harvest truly is plenteous****, but the labourers* *are few; pray ye therefore the Lord of the harvest, that he will send forth labourers into his harvest.*

Psalm 126:5–6—They that sow in tears shall reap in joy. He that goeth forth and weepeth, bearing precious seed, ***shall doubtless come again*** *with rejoicing [**shouts of joy**], bringing his sheaves with him.*

Mark 1:17—And Jesus said unto them, Come ye after me, and ***I will make you*** *to become fishers of men.*

Luke 5:10—And Jesus said . . . Fear not; from henceforth ***thou shalt catch*** *men.*

We are to go through life looking for a harvest. If we can't find a harvest, we can sow, expecting the seeds we sow to produce fruit. We are not trying to "drum up business." We are simply taking God at His word and stepping out in faith.

LESSON 3

ASSIGNMENT SHEET

- ☐ Complete the On the Job Training Debriefing Chart for last week's encounters.
- ☐ Pray with your prayer partners.
- ☐ Read Lesson 3, "Making Friends Through Conversation."
- ☐ Read chapters 7–9 from *Just What the Doctor Ordered.*
- ☐ Memorize 1 John 3:4*b* and Romans 3:23.
- ☐ Memorize Lesson 3 Memory Sheet.
- ☐ Say Lesson 3 Memory Sheet out loud from memory in front of a mirror.
- ☐ Say Lesson 3 Memory Sheet to someone before class.
  Have him check the points you remember, listening for accuracy.
- ☐ Hand out five gospel tracts.
- ☐ Pray for the lost and for God's power on your life.
- ☐ Evaluate your Find Five List, continue to actively pursue reaching the people on it, and add new people as needed.

LESSON 3

ONE-PAGE **MEMORY SHEET**

*"Come and see the works of God. . . . I will declare what he hath done for my soul." (Psalm 66:5*a*, 16*b*)*

☐ **CONVERSATION**
I must turn the conversation to the theme of themes.

☐ ① **Making Conversation**
☐ ② **Directing Conversation**
☐ "How would you describe your relationship with God?"
☐ "What do you think it takes to have a relationship with God and live with Him forever in heaven?"
☐ Personal Testimony—He has changed my life.
☐ "Are you 100% sure that all your sins are forgiven and you will go to heaven?"
☐ 1 John 5:13 or Titus 3:5
☐ "May I show you from the Bible how to have a relationship with God?"

☐ **INTRODUCTION**
I must introduce the sinner to the Savior.

☐ ① **God Is Holy** and cannot tolerate our sin.
☐ **God's Intolerance**—Habakkuk 1:13*a*
☐ **God's Reflection**—1 John 3:4*b*
Ten Commandments
☐ **Man's Dilemma**—Romans 3:23
☐ Illustration—Flagpole

☐ ② **God Is Just** and cannot overlook our sin.

☐ ③ **God Is Loving** and has reached out to us.
☐ He has provided a way for us to be close to Him that satisfies His holy/just nature (John 3:16).

☐ ④ **God Is Gracious** and offers salvation as a gift.

☐ **INVITATION**
I must offer the inquirer the gift of eternal life.

☐ **ASSIMILATION**
I must call the disciple to the life of Christ.

LESSON 3

MAKING FRIENDS THROUGH CONVERSATION

THE FOLLOWING IS DESIGNED TO SHOW A SOUL THE LOVE OF JESUS AND MUST BE DONE IN DEPENDENCE ON THE HOLY SPIRIT.

I. How to carry on a compelling conversation

A. Practical methods for starting conversations at church (Your church lobby may be one of the most productive places to look for people who are open to their need for the gospel.)

1. Show genuine interest and concern.

2. Ask questions like the following.

    - How did you happen to come to our church?
    - Do you know any of our members?
    - How did you enjoy the service?
    - Did you notice anything different about the service or the people?
    - What is your church background?
    - Have you ever heard preaching like that before?
    - Was the Holy Spirit speaking to you (tugging at or squeezing your heart)?
    - How would you describe your relationship with God?

3. If you don't have time to witness at that moment, make an appointment while you are standing face to face. If you don't make an appointment in person at church, visit later in the week unannounced. If it is an inconvenient time, graciously try to make an appointment at the doorstep. You will find that people are very receptive to this.

    Eight or nine out of ten appointments made over the phone end up with negative results.

B. Practical methods for starting conversations in a home

1. The introduction to a conversation is like an airplane at takeoff. It is one of the most critical moments of the whole visit.

   a. On the doorstep

      1) Stand where all the team may be seen but don't stand too close to the door.

      2) Once the door is open, don't line up as three against one. Stand in a circle that includes your new friend in the doorway.

      3) Be friendly and brief.

         a) The longer you visit on the doorstep, the less likely you are to get into the home.

         b) You are much more likely to have a warm conversation that leads to the gospel in the home than on the doorstep.

      4) Emphasize the operative words **"May we come in?"**
      If a team leader is consistently writing "Good doorstep visit" on his visitation report, he probably is not asking, "May we come in?"

      5) Sample doorstep word tracks

      Church visitor
      "Hi, I'm ________ and this is ________. We're from (name of church). You visited our church Sunday, and we stopped by to return the favor. May we come in?"

      Phone-call contact
      "Hello, I'm ________ and this is ________. We're from (name of church). ________ from our church talked to ________ on the phone about giving you some more information about our church. She/he asked us to stop by to chat with you about it. May we come in?"

      Teen-visitation contact
      "Hello, I'm ________ and this is ________. We're from (name of church). One of our teens, ________, was here last week and told us you seem to be interested in our church. He/she asked us to stop by to chat with you. May we come in?"

   b. During the introduction

      1) The mood needs to be somewhat light.

      2) Humor at this point can help relax and change the whole attitude of the person.

      "I don't like organized religion." Response: "Then you'll love our church. We're very disorganized."

      "We're not Baptist." Response: "That's okay! We're not prejudiced."

      3) You're going to be talking about the basic components of your new friend's life.

      - Where he is from
      - What he does
      - His family background
      - His hobbies

2. There are things that make a conversation compelling and draw the person to you.

   a. Show interest by being observant.

      1) Search the room for indications of interests.

      2) People usually put their valued treasures out for you to notice. Notice them.

      3) Look for pictures of the family, toys, type of decor, trophies, pictures on the wall. These not only give you something to say but also reveal the person's interests.

      4) Observe body language.

         - Is he or she nervous?
         - Does the person appear friendly? Lonely?
         - Is the person reserved?

         Keep your mind off **your response** and try to meet the person's needs at the moment.

   b. Ask conversational questions.

      1) To ensure the conversation begins without awkward pauses, avoid questions with yes or no answers.

      2) Ask questions like the following:

         - Where are you from?
         - Where do you work?
         - What do you like about the area?
         - What do you like to do in your spare time?
         - Who have you met in the area?
         - Why did you move here?
         - How do you feel about your move (your school, this part of town, etc.)?

      3) Learn as much as you can about the person. Show genuine interest and concern. If it is a church visit, ask the same questions you would ask a visitor at church.

         - How did you happen to come to our church?
         - Do you know any of our members?
         - How did you enjoy the service?
         - Did you notice anything different about the service or the people?
         - What is your church background?
         - Have you ever heard preaching like that before?
         - Was the Holy Spirit speaking to you (tugging at or squeezing your heart)?
         - How would you describe your relationship with God?

      4) One way of letting a person know you are really interested in him is to ask him how he is doing. When he gives you the obligatory "fine" or "so, so," look straight into his eyes and say, "How are you **really** doing?" Then listen carefully.

   c. Be quiet and listen.

      1) Don't just wait your turn to get a chance to talk. Don't focus on what you are going to say next. Think about your friend. Show genuine interest because you are genuinely interested in him!

2) Earn the right to be heard and demonstrate Christian love.

3) Show him that you are listening.

4) Respond verbally. Try to remember what he says and refer back to it.

5) Respond nonverbally.

- Use body language to communicate that you care about him and what he is saying.

  Sit forward in your chair. Don't cross your arms over your chest.

  Look him in the eye.

  Nod when he makes a point or shares something about himself.

  Match his intensity with yours. If he is calm and laid back, settle down. If he is intense and talkative, step it up a notch.

- Use his name early in the conversation. (He'll like to hear it, and it will help you remember it.)

6) Slowly you will begin to meet the real person and make the conversation warm.

d. Give a sincere compliment.

Proverbs 25:11—A word fitly spoken is like apples of gold in pictures of silver.

Clay Trumbull gives illustration after illustration of using a compliment as a means of opening the way to the gospel.

ROUGH FELLOW

Trumbull told a story of being seated on a train next to a young man with a tell-tale ruddy complexion who twice took a large whiskey bottle out of his suitcase and offered a drink to Trumbull before taking one himself. After the second drink the young man commented, "You must think I'm a pretty rough fellow."

We might have thought this was our opportunity to point out the danger and evil of strong drink, but Mr. Trumbull knew the power of a word fitly spoken and offered the only honest commendation he could: "I think you're a very generous-hearted fellow."

His kind response had drawn the young man to him, allowing an opportunity to give advice. "But I tell you frankly I don't think your whiskey-drinking is the best thing for you."

The young man replied, "Well, I don't believe it is."

With that Trumbull began to find out a little about the man's story. He had left home angry and had made a mess out of his life, but on this trip he was going home for Thanksgiving dinner. The two of them had a friendly conversation that ended with an appeal to entrust himself into the hands of the all-sufficient Savior.

Charles Gallaudet Trumbull, *Taking Men Alive* (New York: Fleming H. Revell Company, 1938), 80–83.

e. Create a desire to hear the gospel.

1) We are the salt of the earth, and Christ is the Water of Life.

2) Listen for a particular need, and show how Christ can fulfill that need.

3) Be sensitive to needs. Everyone has a need!

4) If you find a need, it should be investigated. Show genuine interest and concern.

5) When you give your personal testimony, show the wonders of life in Christ.

6) Share personal details in your testimony. When you open your heart, it will be easier for your new friend to open his heart to your Savior.

C. Practical conversation tips

1. Become a powerful communicator.

a. Only seven percent of most communication is the actual words we say.

b. Thirty-eight percent of communication is vocal production (tone, inflection, compassion).

c. Fifty-five percent of communication is visual (body language, eye contact, gestures, smiles, and, of course, your lifestyle).

2. Eliminate habits that might be offensive or distract from the gospel message.

a. Do not have poor hygiene (bad breath, body odor, unkempt appearance), inappropriate facial expressions (looking bored, scowling), or bad manners (tapping your fingers, watching the clock).

b. Do not talk too much or speak in a monotone voice.

c. Pay close attention to what the other person is saying. Looking away or interrupting someone while he is speaking will communicate that you are not really interested in him.

3. Dress attractively.

a. It is wise to dress stylishly. Consider what a lost person thinks of you when he sees your appearance.

b. Some people need to update their "look."

1 Corinthians 9:19–23—For though I be free from all men, yet have ***I made myself servant unto all, that I might gain the more.*** *And unto the Jews I became as a Jew, that I might gain the Jews; to them that are under the law, as under the law, that I might gain them that are under the law; to them that are without law, as without law, (being not without law to God, but under the law to Christ,) that I might gain them that are without law. To the weak became I as weak, that I might gain the weak:* ***I am made all things to all men, that I might by all means save some.*** *And this I do for the gospel's sake, that I might be partaker thereof with you.*

1) Paul lived as a servant to those around him. He thought more about them than he did himself.

*Philippians 2:3*b—*In lowliness of mind let each esteem other better than themselves.*

2) His objective was to gain more souls.

3) Paul **adjusted himself** to be better suited for ministering to the eternal needs of the lost. For example, if you live in the city, you might have to dress differently than if you live in a rural environment.

4) Some have used these verses to advocate worldliness and sometimes sinfulness. Frankly, that

is counterintuitive for most Spirit-dependent Christians.

c. Look in the mirror and ask yourself how your unsaved counterparts see you. You don't want to appear to be a part of a time-warped group as some have been in the past.

d. Believers can be pure and distinctly Christian without appearing dowdy or unattractive. Our lives are to "adorn the doctrine of God our Saviour in all things" (Titus 2:10*b*).

4. Remember these additional notes regarding conversations in a typical church visit.

   a. The team leader should help arrange the seating.

      1) Avoid seating the entire team on the same couch, creating a "three of us against one of you" situation.

      2) Attempt to create a circular seating arrangement that includes your new friend.

      3) Seat the designated speaker close to the person being visited.

      4) Try to seat your new friend and the speaker kitty-corner from each other.

      5) The kitchen table is probably the most comfortable setting.

   b. All team members should participate in the first part of the visit. Your new friend does not need to know you are following a plan.

      1) When the team leader begins to turn the conversation to spiritual things, the other team members should allow him to do the talking and enter the conversation only when asked by the leader or clearly led by the Holy Spirit.

      2) The "silent partners" are very important.

         a) They can pray (with their eyes open).

         b) They can pay close attention to the conversation and not allow themselves to get distracted by the environment.

         c) They can help deal with distractions. (If they help with children, they should always do so within view of the parents.)

II. The art of making friends and lasting relationships

A. No matter how or when you meet the person, you can count on becoming his friend quickly if you will use the information you have just learned.

B. Jesus said, "The fields . . . are white already to harvest" (John 4:35*b*), but we tend to be blind to the open doors God sets before us.

   1. We can all experience what the Philadelphian church experienced. "I have set before thee an open door" (Revelation 3:8).

   2. We must all beware of the problem of the Laodicean church. "And knowest not that thou art . . . blind" (Revelations 3:17).

Our lukewarm lives cause spiritual blindness!

a. *Revelation 3:18—I counsel thee to buy of me gold tried in the fire, that thou mayest be rich; and white raiment, that thou mayest be clothed, and that the shame of thy nakedness do not appear; and anoint thine eyes with eyesalve, that thou mayest see.*

The only solution to our blindness is to turn to God, but we must be willing to make sacrifices.

Revelation 3:20—Behold, I stand at the door, and knock: if any man hear my voice, and open the door, I will come in to him, and will sup with him, and he with me.

b. *Revelation 3:21*a—*To him that overcometh will I grant to sit with me in my throne.*

God has promised to reward those who are willing to pay the cost and win the lost. We will never regret our work for the kingdom of heaven. Ask God to show you the people He wants you to reach.

1 Corinthians 16:9—For ***a great door and effectual is opened unto me****, and there are many adversaries.*

Do you believe God has given you open doors for the gospel? Are you willing to battle the adversaries? Are you willing to **go**, **find**, and **invite** the lost to "come and see" Jesus?

C. There are many places to look for friends for Jesus. Ask Him to help you cultivate old relationships and develop new relationships into open doors to present the gospel.

1. Redemptive relationships

Develop soulwinning as a natural part of your daily life by asking God to point out the people He is drawing to Himself.

JOHN R. RICE

My father-in-law tells the story of John R. Rice in a crowded lobby in his church in Durango, Colorado. Dr. Rice reached across three people to touch the shoulder of my father-in-law's mailman, whom he had invited to the service. Dr. Rice asked if he knew the Lord, took him into a quiet room, and led him to Christ. Somehow he was aware of the man's need and receptivity. Though he did not have a relationship with him before that encounter, he did after it.

a. Take time to develop relationships with hairdressers, salesmen, clerks, mechanics, and so forth.

b. Work diligently to get to know your neighbors.

c. Network with new believers. Help them share the gospel with their friends.

Show me a new Christian, and I'll show you a large group of possible redemptive relationships.

Feel free to visit one of your personal contacts during On the Job Training. **Remember, your Find Five list is your best source for effective evangelism**. (see page 13)

2. Religious questionnaire evangelism (Find the Religious Questionnaire in the Handout section in this book or at www.exchangemessage.org.)
When going house-to-house (or buzzer-to-buzzer in some apartment or condominium complexes) it is helpful to use this very simple, but effective, questionnaire to find interested people. Some may not prefer this way of finding lost souls, but door-to-door work often provides opportunities to give the

gospel presentation.

3. Phone-call evangelism
   The Phone's for You is a great tool for advertising a large event, but regular phone calling can also provide a steady source of contacts. Get a new move-in list from the phone company that facilitates this. Just call through the list, tell them who you are, and ask if they are interested in information about your church. If so, send a soulwinner to take it to them, rather than mail it.

4. New baby evangelism
   There is something in almost every new mother that causes her to long to help her baby know God. Preparing a gift basket and hand delivering it is a very good way to endear yourself to a young mother. Be sure to include a copy of *The Exchange* Bible study and invite her to do it with you.

5. Church visitor evangelism
   Someone who visits your church has already told you a lot about himself.

   a. I am interested enough to step toward you.

   b. I am open and visiting a fundamental church even though that lifestyle might be alien to me (e.g., traditional music, modest dress, Bible preaching).

   c. It is probable that the Lord is drawing him. Remember, the flesh doesn't seek after God.

      Philippians 1:6—Being confident of this very thing, that ***he which hath begun a good work*** *in you* ***will perform it*** *until the day of Jesus Christ.*

      If we see God's hand beginning something, we can be confident that He will finish it.

Conclusion

"Finding the fish" (the art of finding souls to evangelize) is a term based on the fishing motif Jesus used when He demonstrated that He knew where "the fish" were and would show His disciples where to "fish" if they would follow Him.

*Matthew 4:19*b—*Follow me, and I will make you fishers of men.*

He still knows where "the fish" are and will show us if we are willing to follow Him.

A Singaporean team being trained for soulwinning was out looking for contacts when one of the Singaporeans ran into someone he knew. In typical Asian courtesy, the whole team waited while the two conversed. After they finished and the man was walking away, the Singaporean who had been talking to the man remembered why they were there in the first place. With a beautiful Singaporean accent he cried out in realization, "That's a fish!" He went after him; and in just a matter of time, a new convert had been "caught for life."

SECTION 2

GOSPEL PRESENTATION

LESSON 4

ASSIGNMENT SHEET

- ☐ Complete the On the Job Training Debriefing Chart for last week's encounters.
- ☐ Pray with your prayer partners.
- ☐ Read Lesson 4, "Directing Conversation."
- ☐ Read chapters 10–12 from *Just What the Doctor Ordered.*
- ☐ Memorize Romans 6:23 and Matthew 25:41.
- ☐ Memorize Lesson 4 Memory Sheet.
- ☐ Say Lesson 4 Memory Sheet out loud from memory in front of a mirror.
- ☐ Say Lesson 4 Memory Sheet to someone before class.
  Have him check the points you remember, listening for accuracy.
- ☐ Hand out five gospel tracts.
- ☐ Pray for the lost and for God's power on your life.
- ☐ Evaluate your Find Five List, continue to actively pursue reaching the people on it, and add new people as needed.

LESSON 4

ONE-PAGE **MEMORY SHEET**

"Come and see the works of God. . . . I will declare what he hath done for my soul." (Psalm 66:5a, 16b)

☐ CONVERSATION
I must turn the conversation to the theme of themes.

☐ ① **Making Conversation**
☐ ② **Directing Conversation**
☐ "How would you describe your relationship with God?"
☐ "What do you think it takes to have a relationship with God and live with Him forever in heaven?"
☐ Personal Testimony—He has changed my life.
☐ "Are you 100% sure that all your sins are forgiven and you will go to heaven?"
☐ 1 John 5:13 or Titus 3:5
☐ "May I show you from the Bible how to have a relationship with God?"

☐ INTRODUCTION
I must introduce the sinner to the Savior.

☐ ① **God Is Holy** and cannot tolerate our sin.
☐ **God's Intolerance**—Habakkuk 1:13*a*
☐ **God's Reflection**—1 John 3:4*b*
Ten Commandments
☐ **Man's Dilemma**—Romans 3:23
☐ Illustration—Flagpole

☐ ② **God Is Just** and cannot overlook our sin.
☐ **God's Standard**—Romans 6:23*a*
☐ **God's Judgment**—Matthew 25:41
☐ **Man's Destiny**—Revelation 21:8
☐ Illustration—Judge acquitting a proven murderer/brother
"Would that be justice?"

☐ ③ **God Is Loving** and has reached out to us.
☐ He has provided a way for us to be close to Him that satisfies His holy/just nature (John 3:16).

☐ ④ **God Is Gracious** and offers salvation as a gift.

☐ INVITATION
I must offer the inquirer the gift of eternal life.

☐ ASSIMILATION
I must call the disciple to the life of Christ.

LESSON 4

DIRECTING CONVERSATION

RESOLVE: I MUST TURN THE CONVERSATION TO THE THEME OF THEMES.

from the One-Page Memory Sheet

- ☐ ① Making conversation
- ☐ ② Directing conversation
- ☐ "How would you describe your relationship with God?"
- ☐ "What do you think it takes to have a relationship with God and live with him forever in heaven?"
- ☐ Personal testimony—"He has changed my life."
- ☐ "Are you 100 percent sure that all your sins are forgiven and you will go to heaven?"
- ☐ 1 John 5:13 or Titus 3:5
- ☐ "May I show you from the Bible how to have a relationship with God?"

I. Directing conversations to the theme of themes

A. Ask a question that will turn the conversation to the theme of themes.

1. Bible examples

*John 9:35*b—*Dost thou believe on the Son of God?*

*Acts 8:30*b—*Understandest thou what thou readest?*

2. Modern possibilities

a. Your question can be a topic relevant to the setting.

WALTER WILSON

Walter Wilson was a master at directing conversations. He was in a furniture store looking for a bookcase. The salesperson was walking with him through the chairs to the back of the store when he asked her, "Did you know the most beautiful and expensive building ever built did not have a single chair in it?"

She was astonished to find he was talking about Solomon's Temple and asked him to sit down and tell her why. He explained that there were no chairs because the priests' work was never done. The people kept sinning, and the priests had to continue offering sacrifices. Then he quoted Hebrews 1:3*b*, "When he had by himself purged our sins, sat down on the right hand of the Majesty on high," and began to tell her of the finished work of Jesus on the cross.

Walter L. Wilson, *Just What the Doctor Ordered* (Greenville, SC: BJU Press, 1988), 67–70.

MAN WITH HIV

When a relative of a family in our church was diagnosed with HIV, his mother urged him to talk with me. Sitting in my office, he told me about his diagnosis. We talked about his condition for a while and what kind of treatments the doctors were going to use. After we had talked for some time, and he began to get over the awkwardness of such a visit, I asked him, "What kind of needs have you experienced through this?"

He looked into my eyes with determined earnestness and said, "I want to make sure I'm on my way to heaven!" From there, giving the gospel was a delight, and he was quick to turn to Christ.

We must cultivate the mentality of thinking of ways to direct conversations. When turning a conversation to the gospel, it is usually easier to do a three-point turn than a U-turn. It is unusual for a conversation to go directly to the gospel. It is usually necessary to direct the conversation to spiritual things and from there turn it the rest of the way to the gospel.

Note: As a help to the soulwinner, Scripture passages are in italics and suggested transitions or explanations are marked with a ★. *Giving the Exchange* is designed to be a compelling, conversational-style presentation.

b. Your question can be a topic that relates to religion or church.

★ Do you have a church home in this area?

★ Did you grow up in church?

★ What is your church background?

★ Are you interested in spiritual things?

Use a conversational, friendly tone. Don't let any nervousness on your part make this question become stilted or contrived. This is simply the next question of a warm, caring conversation.

B. Make a statement that will turn the conversation to the theme of themes.

1. Bible examples

*John 3:3*b—*Except a man be born again.*

*John 4:7*b—*Give me to drink.*

2. Modern possibilities

a. Your statement can be something relevant to the situation.

PREMATURE BIRTH

A woman in our church had a sister who gave birth to an extremely tiny, premature baby. At the time she was the smallest baby ever born in Colorado to survive. The new mother asked her sister if she thought I would be willing to come to the hospital to pray for her baby. I met the mother and father in the lobby.

Standing in the busy lobby, they began to tell me what the doctors were telling them, and of their concern for their daughter's life. I simply said to them, "**In a situation like this, you need the Lord!**" With tears streaming down their faces, they nodded. I asked them if we could talk for a little bit before we went up to see the baby. There were a few chairs in a corner next to the windows, and I suggested we sit down. I began asking questions about their spiritual condition, discovering that the mother knew the Lord but the young father probably didn't. I asked if I could show him from the Bible Who God is and how to have a personal relationship with Him. He quickly agreed and was wonderfully saved.

b. Your statement can be a topic that relates to religion or church.

★ "The other day at church . . ."

★ "While I was reading my Bible, I found a passage that stated . . ."

It is not necessary to turn the conversation directly to the gospel. Simply directing the conversation to spiritual topics makes it easy to ask the person about his relationship with God and proceed from there to the gospel.

C. Some conversations are easier to turn than others.

1. Jesus watched for opportunities to turn conversations to the theme of themes. He used the following:

   a. Water—John 4

   b. Bread—John 6

   c. Light—John 9

   d. Death—John 11

2. All people go through times of calm and times of crisis, times of resistance and times of responsiveness. Difficulty and change tend to make people receptive.

   Be alert—express loving concern at such times.

   Be prepared—"learn of his [or her] need, and, if possible, meet it."

   a. The Thomas Holmes Psychological Stress Scale shows, on a scale of 1 to 100, the degree of receptivity when faced with the following:

      Death of a spouse 100
      Divorce or separation 73
      Loss of job 47
      Change of residence 20

   b. Find a need and meet it. Find a hurt and heal it.

      Job 36:15—He delivereth the poor in his affliction, and openeth their ears in oppression.

3. The following types of conversations can easily be turned to the theme of themes.

   a. A conversation about a close call with death

      Death naturally opens the door to talk about eternity. When talking about death, we must always use sensitivity and tact. Even Jesus did not name the rich man who was in hell, though he did name Lazarus, who was in paradise.

   b. A conversation about a tragic news headline

      Tragedy (bad news) can lead to a discussion of good news. We can lead the conversation to this thought, "At a time like that, people really need the Lord."

   c. A friend's request that you pray about something

      He is evidencing an interest in spiritual things. You can ask if your friend feels he is on "praying ground." Explain that to be on praying ground he must know God personally. Then ask if you can introduce him to God and show him how to have a relationship with God.

   d. Opportunities from your life's story that communicate the impact of your relationship with God

      1) your church

      2) your *Giving the Exchange* training

      3) the Bible

      4) your childhood

      5) how you met your spouse

   e. Converations centered on special holidays or seasons of the year that lend themselves to directing a conversation to God

      1) Valentine's Day—How much God loves us or the fact that all love ultimately points back to Him

      2) Easter—The resurrection of Christ

      3) Fourth of July—Freedom in Christ or our Christian heritage

      4) Christmas—The birth of Christ

      5) Birthday—Second birth

      Use your own ideas. Watch for the open doors God is placing in your path.

II. Asking the first question

How would you describe your relationship with God?

A. Ask this question as naturally as anything else you have asked. (Remember, you are acquiring a friend.)

B. From the very first question of the *Giving the Exchange* Gospel Presentation, aim at making the encounter a **conversation**, not a **monologue**.

   1. This question will establish that precedent. Be sure to respond to the specifics of the person's answers.

2. You will find that no matter how he responds, the answer will pave the way to tell him about the wonders of your personal relationship with God.

C. This question turns the conversation quickly and sets the tone for a serious introduction to Who God is and how to have a vibrant relationship with Him.

If you have taken time to show genuine care and concern for your new friend, you will be surprised at how effective this question is in finishing the turn toward the gospel.

ON THE FRITZ

A repairman came to our home one day. When he was finished, I went out to discuss the work he had done and to pay him. I began to turn the conversation by asking him if he went to church anywhere. When he responded, I continued the turn by asking him how he would describe his relationship with God. His answer was "It's on the fritz right now."

I asked him what was wrong, and he told me that his wife had just left him and that he was trying to figure out what to do. It was apparent he was not living a very happy life. I told him that my relationship with God was very real to me and that He gave me comfort from His Word on a daily basis. He replied, "That's what I need."

We didn't have time to continue the conversation right then, but I asked him if we could do *The Exchange* Bible study. We set up a time and met for lunch the next day.

It is amazing what people tell me about themselves when I have taken a few minutes to begin our relationship with friendship and then ask this question.

D. If you listen carefully you will learn much from their answer.

1. You will learn *by the zeal* they use to describe their relationship.

2. You will learn *by the ease* (or lack thereof) of their description.

3. You will begin to learn their needs *by the words* they use to describe their relationship with God.

III. Asking the diagnostic questions

A. **Diagnostic question 1:**
What do you think it takes to have a relationship with God and live with Him forever in heaven?

1. Sometimes your friend won't know how to answer.

   a. The answer to this question is essential to understanding your friend's need.

   b. Sometimes simply asking, "What do you **think**?" solves the problem.

   c. Here are some other ways to ask this question if your friend gets stuck.

   - "If someone you loved asked you how to know they were going to heaven, what would you tell them?"
   - "If you came upon a scene where someone was near death and asked you how to get to heaven, what would you tell him?"
   - "If you were to stand before God and He were to ask you, 'Why should I let you into My

heaven?' what would you say?"

2. Once your friend has answered, ask, "Anything else?"

   a. If he has given a "works-type" answer, this simple question sometimes begins to demonstrate the shallowness of his answer.

   b. If he gives a vague "faith" answer, this will help you get more specific.

   c. Many people in the American culture have a split trust between Jesus and their own works. It is important to know this so you can deal with it later.

   Note: If you don't get this information now, you may go through the whole introduction to God and have your friend tell you, "Oh, I've already done that." If you suspect he has split trust and is not really saved, this information will enable you to help him understand this problem when you get to the invitation.

3. This is the first of two diagnostic questions. **You will need the answers to both this question and the second diagnostic question to accurately diagnose your friend's spiritual condition**.

   a. If he answers the "what do you think it takes" question wrong and answers the next "100 percent sure" question with "Yes, I am 100 percent sure," then you will assume he has a **false assurance** of salvation and can deal with him accordingly.

   b. If he answers the "what do you think it takes" question correctly (some form of "Jesus' finished work on the cross") but answers the "100 percent sure" question with "I hope so," you can investigate to see if there has been a **genuine salvation** experience and deal with it accordingly.

   c. If you ask one of these questions without the other, you will get an incomplete understanding of your friend's condition and might not be able to meet his real need.

      1) He may be saved and just not have assurance or know how to express it. (I've met many people who think it is haughty to say that they are 100 percent sure.)

      2) Your friend may think he is safe but may actually be depending on something other than Jesus. In this case you have to know and do your best to warn him of his need.

      Note: Your personal testimony comes after the first diagnostic question and paves the way for the second diagnostic question.

B. **Diagnostic question 2:**
Are you 100 percent sure that all your sins are forgiven and that you're going to heaven?

1. The answer that is easiest to deal with is "no" or anything less than 100 percent.

   a. Emphasize "100 percent" when you ask the question to bring out any doubt he might have.

   b. A "no" answer is often a great sign that the Lord is about to use you in this soul's eternal destiny.

      1) Show him this Bible truth:

      *1 John 5:13*a—*These things have I written . . . that* ***ye may know that ye have eternal life***.

      2) Go directly to the final question.

Note: The information you learned from the "what do you think it takes" question will be very helpful to you as you introduce your friend to God and show him how God has met his need.

2. The most common answer is some form of "**maybe/I hope so/I'd like to think so**."

   a. It is easy to simply say, "You seem to have some doubt. Do you know the Bible says we can know? In fact, God told us He wants us to know."

   b. Show him 1 John 5:13 and proceed to the final question.

3. The hardest combination of answers is when a person answers the "what do you think it takes" question wrong and the "100 percent sure" question with "Yes."

   a. If your friend's answer to the "what do you think it takes" question was **works** related, show him this Bible truth:

      *Titus 3:5*a—***Not by works*** *of righteousness* ***which we have done****, but according to his mercy he saved us.*

      ★ Then kindly say, "That's different from what you just told me. Let me show you what the Bible teaches about how to have a relationship with God."

      This may seem rather direct, but you will never get a chance to introduce him to the answer if you don't expose his need.

   b. If his answer to the "what do you think it takes" question is **faith** in God or Jesus **plus works**, then show him this Bible truth:

      Romans 3:28—Therefore we conclude that a man is justified ***by faith without the deeds*** *of the law.*

      ★ Then say, "That's different from what you just told me. May I show you from the Bible how to have a relationship with God?"

IV. Giving a salvation testimony

You have asked the person about his relationship with God, now tell him about yours.

A. Your testimony **must be brief**.

   1. When it is written, your testimony should not be longer than one page.

   2. When spoken, it should not be long enough to dominate the conversation.

   3. Sometimes I don't take time to give much of my testimony. Like the story above, I just give evidence of the reality and value of my relationship with God.

B. Your testimony **must be a story**.

   1. Most of us tend to make theologically correct statements about how we know we are saved but never tell our story.

a. We have learned to give our testimony to other believers, trying to convince them that we are saved.

b. **We must learn to give our testimony to unbelievers**. They need to hear why we began our relationship with God and what kind of change it has made.

2. The actual telling of your story will demonstrate that God is a real person and is working in real time today.

a. Be transparent and personal. This will open the conversation so that your friend will be drawn to you and feel more comfortable being open and personal with you.

b. If your relationship with God is warm and inviting, it will help create a thirst in your friend's heart for that kind of intimate relationship with God!

1) You've heard it said, "You can lead a horse to water, but you can't make him drink." You can't make him drink, but you can make him thirsty by giving him salt.

*Matthew 5:13*a—***Ye are*** *the* ***salt*** *of the earth.*

Colossians 4:6—***Let your speech be*** *alway with grace,* ***seasoned with salt****, that ye may know how ye ought to answer every man.*

2) Ask God to enable you by grace to make your testimony compelling, thereby causing people to thirst for the Water of Life.

3. Avoid religious or theological words that only Christians know, for example, *saved, lost, rededicate, sanctified, justified.* These tend to confuse and alienate people.

C. Every testimony should include three things.

1. The negative condition of your life without Christ

a. Everyone senses his need for Christ differently. Some are close to suicide, some hear a message on hell and are afraid, some simply sense a deep longing and emptiness, and so forth.

b. You may have to work at this, but remember what led you to understand your need for Christ and simply **tell your story**.

c. Expect to strike a harmonious chord in the heart of your friend.

1) God created every human with a **God-shaped hole** in his heart.

KARLTON

I first met Karlton on a vacation Bible school visit. He had been to church a few times but had never filled out a guest registration card. When I finally got contact information through VBS registration, I still couldn't get anyone to answer the door when my wife and I tried to visit. My wife had met his wife at VBS and persisted to reach her by phone, eventually setting an appointment for us to come to their home. When I asked Karlton about his relationship with God he asked me, "So, do I have to believe in this Adam and Eve stuff to have a relationship with this God of yours?"

He felt God was a figment of weak men's imagination. I answered that I understood how someone sitting on the outside looking in would think that but asked him to suppose for a moment that there really was a God and that He had created men with a God-shaped hole in their hearts so that they would look for Him. I suggested that people often try to fill that void with sin and material things and even human relationships, but only an intimate relationship with God will satisfy the deep needs of the heart.

While doing *The Exchange* Bible study with him, I discovered that though he had filled his life with everything he had ever dreamed of—a good wife, a nice home, a great job, and even adoring children—he had not found the satisfaction he thought these would bring. This need made him open to investigate the Bible's claims about Who God is. Though he approached lesson 1 with the same skepticism of our first visit, lesson 2 was different. His questions were more sincere and inquiring than skeptical. Before we were able to do lesson 3, he accepted Christ.

Here is a postcard I received from him a year later.

> Dear Jeff and Anna,
>
> Hello from Seattle where although I am on business and away from home and my family, I'm celebrating my first year anniversary of salvation and knowing the Lord. I want to thank you for your love and passion for the Lord and your genuine willingness to teach others such as myself. I truly believe that God knew it would take you to stir my heart and lead me in the direction of the Lord and His will. This past year has been a wonderful time with true purpose.
>
> Karlton

2) **If your friend is lost, there is something missing in his life**. You can expect the Holy Spirit to use your story to remind him of his need.

d. If you were too young to remember the negative condition of your life without Christ, focus on the next two parts of your testimony.

   It is not necessary to say the specific age when you received Christ. It is difficult for an adult to relate to someone who experienced conversion at a very young age, and mentioning your age tends to alienate some people.

2. The story of the moment you received eternal life

   a. Everyone comes to Christ the same way—by faith.

      You should not give the gospel at this point. (You'll do that later.)

   b. It is necessary to point out that there was a specific time when you received Christ.

   c. Be clear about what changed your life. Don't let it sound like works or a process, rather a gift you received.

      This does not need to be more than a sentence or two.

3. The reality of the transformation God has made (and is making) in your life

   a. If you are saved, you should have a changed life.

      2 Corinthians 5:17—Therefore if any man be in Christ, he is a new creature: old things are passed away; behold, ***all things are become new****.*

When we know Christ intimately, He makes a difference in our lives. Find those places and share them with your friend.

b. **Tell a real story** that demonstrates the change Christ has made in your life! If you were saved as a child, you may want to choose an incident in your adult life in which the Lord made a real difference.

c. This is a testimonial, **an advertisement for the Lord.**

d. Show the wonders of life in Christ.

e. Share personal details. When you open your heart, it is easier for your new friend to open his heart to your Savior.

D. Use your testimony as an opportunity to knock out crutches that people use to avoid the gospel.

1. Private matter—If you thought religion was a private matter that shouldn't be talked about freely, but now you're glad someone had the courage to talk to you about it, say so!

2. Good enough—If you thought that your good living or good works were enough to get you to heaven, say so!

3. Other crutches—Mention anything that was holding you back that you think might be holding others back from receiving Christ.

E. Your testimony will pave the way to the second diagnostic question.

Note: See sample testimonies at the end of lesson 4.

V. Asking the final question:

May I show you from the Bible how to have a relationship with God?

All of this discussion should be very conversational.

A. Get your Bible or your Gospel Presentation System (GPS) out while you are saying this!

The GPS is a four-page, full-color flip chart for the *Giving the Exchange* Gospel Presentation. It keeps you from getting lost while giving the gospel. You can find it at www.exchangemessage.org.

B. If he says he is too busy, attempt to make an appointment. We live in an appointment world, so you will have a better chance of getting in if you make an appointment.

C. If he says he is not interested, at least leave a good gospel tract with him.

SAMPLE TESTIMONY

I was twenty-one when I met a preacher who bought a car from me. His whole family—three little boys, a baby girl, and a sweet wife—came to the dealership to pick it out. Something wholesome about that family made me hungry inside. The life I was living was filled with sin and emptiness. It was just like a saying I heard about beer: "One is too many, and 100,000 is not enough." Every sin I committed was driving me deeper into ruin, but I couldn't seem to get enough and kept chasing it harder and harder.

When the preacher and his family came to pick up their car, one of his little boys cried out, "My daddy's going to ask you to lunch." When we went to lunch, he brought a Bible with him that seemed to fill the table. He started telling me about Jesus and how to have a personal relationship with Him. I felt like everyone in the restaurant was staring at me. When he asked me if I wanted to receive Christ for myself, I was embarrassed and asked if we could do it in the car.

I can still tell you exactly where we were when I bowed my head and prayed a simple prayer to receive Jesus. I had no idea a person's life could change as much as mine has. I hadn't cried since I was twelve years old, but now my heart is filled with such joy and compassion for others I can't help but cry. Slowly the sins of my life slipped away, and real strength and victory have come in their place. Oh, I'm not perfect by any means, but God has changed my heart so much that now I want to do what is right. I'm happily married, have four sweet children of my own, and my relationship with God is still growing.

Let me ask you another question. Are you 100% sure that all of your sins are forgiven and that you will go to heaven?

MY TESTIMONY

I was young when I received Christ, and I don't remember a lot about my life before Him. I do remember wondering about my relationship with God. Once I settled the issue with Him, He began to make a wonderful impact on my life that continues to grow. I feel His guidance and strength on a daily basis. I also have a sense of security about my life and even what will happen to me after I die. No one ever knows exactly how he will face death, but a few years ago I had an opportunity to get about as close as I want to get.

I was traveling west on I-70 into the mountains. I was late for a meeting and was driving too fast. I had my cruise control set on 70 mph and had just tapped my brakes to turn off the cruise control as I turned onto the exit. It was a long off ramp, and a frontage road crossed it. I saw the large van approaching the stop sign, but knowing I had the right of way and trusting the van to stop, I hurried through the intersection. The driver hadn't seen me and pulled out in front of me. All I could do was stomp on my brakes and slam into the side of the big van. My little Ford Tempo ended up in a field next to the road with steam pouring out of the engine. I was afraid the car was going to catch on fire, so I tried to get out. The door was jammed. I realized I was hurt when I tried to crawl over to the other side. I finally managed to get out, but all I could do was lie in the field looking up into the sky, waiting for help. All the while I lay there and even in the ambulance, I had an overwhelming sense of peace and calm. I knew that if I died right then I would go to heaven to live with God.

Let me ask you another question. Are you 100% sure that all of your sins are forgiven and that you will go to heaven?

LESSON 5

ASSIGNMENT SHEET

- ☐ Complete the On the Job Training Debriefing Chart for last week's encounters.
- ☐ Pray with your prayer partners.
- ☐ Read Lesson 5, "God Is Holy and cannot tolerate our sin."
- ☐ Read chapters 13–15 from *Just What the Doctor Ordered.*
- ☐ Watch the *Giving the Exchange* Gospel Presentation Video at www.exchangemessage.org.
- ☐ Memorize Revelation 21:8 and John 3:16.
- ☐ Memorize Lesson 5 Memory Sheet.
- ☐ Say Lesson 5 Memory Sheet out loud from memory in front of a mirror.
- ☐ Say Lesson 5 Memory Sheet to someone before class.
  Have him check the points you remember, listening for accuracy.
- ☐ Hand out five gospel tracts.
- ☐ Pray for the lost and for God's power on your life.
- ☐ Evaluate your Find Five List, continue to actively pursue reaching the people on it, and add new people as needed.

LESSON 5

ONE-PAGE **MEMORY SHEET**

*"Come and see the works of God. . . . I will declare what he hath done for my soul." (Psalm 66:5*a*, 16*b*)*

☐ CONVERSATION

I must turn the conversation to the theme of themes.

☐ ① **Making Conversation**
☐ ② **Directing Conversation**
☐ "How would you describe your relationship with God?"
☐ "What do you think it takes to have a relationship with God and live with Him forever in heaven?"
☐ Personal Testimony—He has changed my life.
☐ "Are you 100% sure that all your sins are forgiven and you will go to heaven?"
☐ 1 John 5:13 or Titus 3:5
☐ "May I show you from the Bible how to have a relationship with God?"

☐ INTRODUCTION

I must introduce the sinner to the Savior.

☐ ① **God Is Holy** and cannot tolerate our sin.
☐ **God's Intolerance**—Habakkuk 1:13*a*
☐ **God's Reflection**—1 John 3:4*b*
Ten Commandments
☐ **Man's Dilemma**—Romans 3:23
☐ Illustration—Flagpole

☐ ② **God Is Just** and cannot overlook our sin.
☐ **God's Standard**—Romans 6:23*a*
☐ **God's Judgment**—Matthew 25:41
☐ **Man's Destiny**—Revelation 21:8
☐ Illustration—Judge acquitting a proven murderer/brother
"Would that be justice?"

☐ ③ **God Is Loving** and has reached out to us.
☐ He has provided a way for us to be close to Him that satisfies His holy/just nature (John 3:16).
☐ **God's Son**
☐ "Who would you say Jesus is?"
God in flesh—John 1:14
☐ **God's Exchange**—Jesus becomes
☐ Our Substitute—1 Peter 3:18
☐ Our Righteousness—2 Corinthians 5:21
☐ Illustration—My record/His record chart
☐ Our Full Payment—1 John 1:7*b*; John 19:30
☐ **Man's Deliverance** from sin and its penalty —1 Corinthians 15:3–4

☐ ④ **God Is Gracious** and offers salvation as a gift.

☐ INVITATION

I must offer the inquirer the gift of eternal life.

☐ ASSIMILATION

I must call the disciple to the life of Christ.

LESSON 5

GOD IS HOLY AND CANNOT TOLERATE SIN

INTRODUCTION TO GOD AS A PERSON

RESOLVE: I MUST INTRODUCE THE SINNER TO THE SAVIOR.

The Bible teaches that God is a person. Some in our culture have come to think of God as a force of nature or an energy source. God is indeed a force with Whom to be reckoned and the greatest power in the universe, but He is so much more than that. If your friend has removed the concept of God's personhood from his thinking, he is damaging his ability to have a real understanding of God and His personal relationships with men.

Apologetics is the discipline of defending biblical truth through the systematic use of reason and logic. It is a wonderful encouragement and certainly has a place in evangelism, but **it is a mistake to depend on apologetics to the exclusion of the clear articulation of Bible truth**.

Mark 4:14–15—The sower soweth the word. And these are they by the way side, where the word is sown; but when they have heard, Satan cometh immediately, and taketh away the word that was sown in their hearts.

Jesus taught that **the Word** is seed that **produces life**, and **the heart is the place of ministry**. Notice that the Word produces life in every heart in which it lodges. It is so powerful that Satan attempts to pluck it out of even the hardest hearts.

Using an apologetic approach instead of carefully presenting Bible truth creates two problems. First, we tend to depend on human logic when God has promised to use His Word. Second, we miss the target of the heart when we aim at the mind. Education is not the answer. The Holy Spirit's conviction is. There is certainly nothing wrong with apologetics, but we dare not allow it to take the place of a simple explanation of the Bible while expecting the Holy Spirit to use the Word to convince your friend of its veracity.

John 16:8—And when he [the Holy Spirit] is come, ***he will reprove*** *[convict or convince] the world of sin, and of righteousness, and of judgment.*

Romans 10:17—So then ***faith cometh by hearing****, and hearing by* ***the word of God****.*

Hebrews 4:12—For the ***word of God*** *is quick, and powerful, and sharper than any twoedged sword, piercing even to the dividing asunder of soul and spirit, and of the joints and marrow, and is a discerner of the thoughts and intents of the heart.*

Isaiah 55:11—So shall my word be that goeth forth out of my mouth: ***it shall not return*** *unto me* ***void****, but it shall accomplish that which I please, and it shall prosper in the thing whereto I sent it.*

*Romans 1:16*a*—For I am not ashamed of* ***the gospel*** *of Christ: for* ***it is the power of God unto salvation*** *to every one that believeth.*

Jeremiah 23:29—Is not ***my word*** *like as* ***a fire****? saith the Lord; and like a hammer that breaketh the rock in pieces?*

Notice how God introduces Himself in the Bible.

Genesis 1:1—In the beginning God created the heaven and the earth.

John 1:1—In the beginning was the Word, and the Word was with God, and the Word was God.

He presupposes, or simply announces, His existence and begins to demonstrate His character. This quotation from *The Exchange* Bible study reminds us of God's purpose for giving us His Word. "The Bible is a series of books from God to men in which He reveals Himself to mankind so that we may know Him." We can use the Bible with confidence, knowing God will speak through us. I like to think of it as handing the Holy Spirit His sword.

It is imperative to ask your new friend questions.

POSSIBLE TRANSITION STATEMENT

★ God is a person. In order to know anyone, you have to know a little bit about him before you can hope to have a relationship with him. Let me introduce you to four simple truths about God so that you can know Him for yourself.

from the One-Page Memory Sheet

☐ ① **God Is Holy** and cannot tolerate our sin.
God says, *"Be ye holy; for I am holy." (1 Peter 1:16*b*)*
☐ **God's Intolerance**—Habakkuk 1:13*a*
☐ **God's Reflection**—1 John 3:4*b*
☐ Ten Commandments
☐ **Man's Dilemma**—Romans 3:23
☐ Illustration—Flagpole

★ The word *holy* means "separate or unique." There is no one like God. He is totally set apart from everyone. One of the implications of His holy nature is that He is totally set apart from sin. He is perfect!

★ God's holiness is referred to as "beautiful" multiple times in Scripture. His holiness is the very essence of His glorious, majestic person. The words holy or holiness are used in connection with God's name over forty times in the Bible. (His name is never associated in this fashion with His justice, love, or grace.)

Isaiah 6:1–5—In the year that king Uzziah died I saw also ***the Lord sitting upon a throne, high and lifted up****, and* ***his train filled the temple****. Above it stood the seraphims [a type of angel]: each one had six wings; with twain he covered his face, and with twain he covered his feet, and with twain he did fly. And one cried unto another, and said,* ***Holy, holy, holy, is the Lord of hosts: the whole earth is full of his glory****. And the posts of the door moved at the voice of him that cried, and the house was filled with smoke.* ***Then said I, Woe is me! for I am undone; because I am a man of unclean lips****, and I dwell in the midst of a people of unclean lips: for* ***mine eyes have seen the King, the Lord of hosts****.*

When men see the holiness of God, they fall at His feet in conviction and awe.

ROBIN

Anna had decided that she would always have *The Exchange* Bible study going with someone at all times, but she had run out of contacts. For a year she had been praying for Robin, a friend of a woman in her Sunday school class. Robin had fought with cancer and had recently been declared cancer-free. Anna asked for her phone number and called her to ask if she would like to do a four-lesson Bible study that would help her be sure she was on her way to heaven. Though they had never met, Robin said yes. Anna drove to her house, gave her the book, and set a time for the next week to discuss lesson 1.

When they met, Robin had her Bible study completed and the book filled out. Anna started the lesson by asking Robin what she thought of the Bible study so far. She responded the way we all should by saying, "**God is awesome!**"

After lesson 4 Robin had assurance that a decision she had made a few years previously was genuine and that based on God's Word she was on her way to heaven. Little did either of them know that within a few short months Robin, who was in her thirties, would be in heaven. Her cancer returned, something went wrong in chemotherapy, and she was gone. She is gone from the pain and the suffering of this world and is personally experiencing the beauty of His holiness.

★ Another word used in close association with His holiness is *righteousness*. The idea is "completely or perfectly fulfilling a contract." You can count on the fact that God will always do the right thing. He is perfectly righteous. There may be times when we do not think that what He is doing is right, but He is holy—we are not. He always does what is right. Not only is He the ruler of all and not answerable to you and me, but also He will always do the right thing. He has to. It is His character—His nature—to do so, and **He cannot violate His nature**.

I. God's intolerance

*Habakkuk 1:13*a—*Thou art of purer eyes than to behold evil, and canst not look on iniquity [sin].*

★ One of the aspects of God's holiness is not just that He dislikes sin but that He cannot tolerate it. It is not that He will not but that He cannot. **He cannot deny any part of His perfect nature**.

EXTRA VERSES THAT MIGHT BE HELPFUL

Matthew 5:48—Be ye therefore perfect, even as your Father which is in heaven is perfect.

Holy is a religious word that seems to escape our comprehension, but somehow we understand the word *perfect*. God is perfect and cannot tolerate our moral imperfections.

Isaiah 64:6—But we are all as an unclean thing, and ***all our righteousnesses [good things] are as filthy rags****; and we all do fade as a leaf; and our iniquities [sins], like the wind, have taken us away.*

II. God's reflection

★ You may struggle with the word *sin*. Many people define right and wrong differently. Knowing God as a person clarifies some of these things. The Bible shows us God's definition of sin.

1. *1 John 3:4*b—*Sin is the* ***transgression [breaking] of the law****.*

   ★ Sin is not defined by my thoughts or by yours. It is defined by God's holy nature. When we sin, we do not simply hurt someone or something; we offend God's holy nature.

2. The Ten Commandments are a reflection of God's holy nature.

   a. God's laws are not arbitrary rules that He has set to "hem us in." They are a reflection of His nature.

      ILLUSTRATION

      A friend of mine has a child with a severe allergy to peanuts. If she eats one peanut or even something fried in peanut oil, she might die. They have very strict rules in their house about peanuts. If you want to have a relationship with them, you have to abide by those rules because they reflect the needs of their family.

   b. We all have to deal with our inability to keep God's laws if we want to have a relationship with Him, because His laws are a reflection of His character.

      Exodus 20: 1–17—And God spake all these words, saying, I am the Lord thy God . . .

      - *Thou shalt have no other gods before me.*
      - *Thou shalt not make unto thee any graven image, or any likeness of any thing that is in heaven above, or that is in the earth beneath, or that is in the water under the earth: thou shalt not bow down thyself to them, nor serve them: for I the Lord thy God am a jealous God, visiting the iniquity [sin] of the fathers upon the children unto the third and fourth generation of them that hate me; and shewing mercy unto thousands of them that love me, and keep my commandments.*
      - *Thou shalt not take the name of the Lord thy God in vain; for the Lord will not hold him guiltless that taketh his name in vain.*
      - *Remember the sabbath day, to keep it holy. Six days shalt thou labour, and do all thy work: but the seventh day is the sabbath of the Lord thy God: in it thou shalt not do any work.*
      - *Honour thy father and thy mother: that thy days may be long upon the land which the Lord thy God giveth thee.*
      - *Thou shalt not kill.*
      - *Thou shalt not commit adultery.*
      - *Thou shalt not steal.*
      - *Thou shalt not bear false witness [lie] against thy neighbour.*
      - *Thou shalt not covet thy neighbor's house, thou shalt not covet thy neighbour's wife, nor his man-servant, nor his maidservant, nor his ox, nor his ass [donkey], nor any thing that is thy neighbour's.*

      Note: When you are doing a Bible study with your friend, dealing with all the Ten Commandments is appropriate. If you are doing a one-time gospel presentation, **choose two or three to ask about**. The key is to allow the Holy Spirit to bring conviction into your friend's heart.

      1) *"Thou shalt have no other gods before me."* The first commandment reflects God's holiness or His unique nature.

      2) *"Thou shalt not make unto thee any graven image . . . Thou shalt not bow down thyself to them."* God's jealous love demands that we have no idols (anything more important to us than God) in our life. This jealousy is not the petty emotion that each of us deals with from time to time but a powerful love that demands loyalty from the loved one.

3) *"Thou shalt not take the name of the Lord thy God in vain."* To take God's name in vain is to use it flippantly or as an expletive, such as in "Oh my _____!"

★ I remember a time when I did that. I was so disappointed with myself! Have you ever done that?

★ **We offended God's holy nature when we broke His law**.

★ What do you think "the Lord will not hold him guiltless" means?

Often when you ask these questions, your friend will look away or down when he answers. What is that? **Conviction**! The Holy Spirit is using His sword to convince the hearer of his need.

*Galatians 3:24*a—*Wherefore the law was our schoolmaster to bring us unto Christ.*

- **Be specific**. If you just say you know we've all sinned and move on, you'll rob the Holy Spirit of the opportunity to convict.
- **Be patient**. We don't bring conviction; the Holy Spirit does. Hand Him His sword through speaking His Word and get out of the way.

John 16:8–9—And when he [the Holy Spirit] is come, he will reprove [convict or convince] the world of sin, and of righteousness, and of judgment: of sin, because they believe not on me.

Conviction is a wonderful thing. Without conviction, men and women can go through life oblivious to their need. When you are used of the Holy Spirit to bring conviction into a life through the Word of God, you are allowing Him to fulfill one of His main objectives in the world!

4) *"Remember the sabbath day, to keep it holy."* God's day is to be hallowed because we respect Him as holy.

5) *"Honour thy father and thy mother."* God created the family to teach us how to love and respect Him through learning to love and respect our parents.

★ How would you define "Honor your father and mother"? To honor is not just obedience, but having and displaying a sweet spirit at all times.

★ I don't know if there has ever been a teenager who hasn't broken that one. Has there ever been a time that you've dishonored your mother or father?

★ **You offended God's holy nature when you broke His law**.

6) *"Thou shalt not kill."* God's command not to **murder** is a reflection of His love for human life. He created and sustains all that lives.

Colossians 1:16–17—For by him were all things created, that are in heaven, and that are in earth, visible and invisible, . . . all things were created by him, and for him: and he is before all things, and by him all things consist.

7) *"Thou shalt not commit adultery."* God's command not to **commit adultery** is a reflection of His devotion to His own personal relationships with men and His commitment to the institution of marriage.

★ I don't ask if the person has committed adultery, but I always strive to mention it. This is a common sin in our culture, and the Holy Spirit uses it to bring conviction.

Hebrews 13:4—Marriage is honourable in all, and the bed undefiled: but whoremongers [people who indulge in sex before marriage] and adulterers God will judge.

God seems to bring a strong sense of guilt and long-term impact from this sin. Touching on it allows the Holy Spirit to deal with it so He can set the person free from it.

8) *"Thou shalt not steal."* God's command not to **steal** shows Him as the provider of all material blessings.

*Matthew 5:45*b—*Your Father which is in heaven . . . maketh his sun to rise on the evil and on the good, and sendeth rain on the just and on the unjust.*

★ Have you ever taken anything that wasn't yours?

★ **You've broken God's law. You've offended His holy nature**.

9) *"Thou shalt not bear false witness [**lie**]."* God's command not to lie reflects His truthful nature.

In fact, Titus 1:2 states that God cannot lie!

*Numbers 23:19*a—*God is not a man, that he should lie.*

★ I read a statistic once that reported that the average American lies sixteen times a day. I don't think I'm that bad, but I have stretched the truth before or told a story in a way that I made myself appear better than I really am. In fact, I've flat-out lied. Have you ever told a lie or stretched the truth?

★ **We've broken God's law. We've offended His holy nature**.

Note: **Always ask about this one**. Everyone has lied, and it will set up the discussion that will be generated later from Revelations 21:8, "And all liars, shall have their part in the lake which burneth with fire."

- A few people have told me that they have never lied, but they were lying! I just kept asking questions until they admitted it.

10) *"Thou shalt not covet."* God's command not to **covet** shows that He holds us responsible for what is in our hearts as well as what is in our conduct.

★ Have you ever found yourself dissatisfied with your current situation and coveted something more than God has chosen to give you? I know I have.

★ **We've broken God's law. We've offended His holy nature**.

EXTRA VERSES THAT MIGHT BE HELPFUL

Matthew 5:48—Be ye therefore perfect, even as your Father which is in heaven is perfect.

*Revelation 21:27*a—*And there shall in no wise enter into it [heaven] any thing that defileth, neither whatsoever worketh abomination, or maketh a lie.*

★ All this leaves us with a dilemma.

III. Man's dilemma

Romans 3:23—For all have sinned, and come short of the glory of God.

A. Even though most people will acknowledge that they have sinned, some still think they are good enough to get to heaven. Point out to your friend that he has come short of the glory of God. God's standard is perfection; and though he may be **very** good, **he is not perfect**!

Ecclesiastes 7:20—For there is not a just man upon earth, that doeth good, and sinneth not.

B. God cannot allow us into heaven with sin in our lives. Heaven is perfect. If we went there with sin, it wouldn't be heaven anymore.

★ How many sins did it take to ruin paradise? Only one! All the sin, pain, and ugliness of this world came from that one sin.

ILLUSTRATION

Flagpole: An analogy that illustrates this might be something as simple as trying to touch the top of a thirty-foot flagpole. You may be able to jump higher than I can, but neither of us can jump that high. We will both come short of the top. The glory of God is His holy standard of perfection. Some might be better than others, but none of us is perfect, and all of us come short.

WOMAN ON AN AIRPLANE

A woman sitting next to me on an airplane took offense to God calling her a sinner. She misunderstood. She thought He was saying she was "really bad," and she knew she was a very good woman. That wasn't the point. The point is that God is "really good!" His perfect nature cannot tolerate even one sin, and we have all committed many more than one. When I quoted Ecclesiastes 7:20 and reminded her that she and I knew a lot of really good people, but neither of us knew anyone who was perfect, she understood and said she agreed.

POSSIBLE TRANSITION STATEMENT

★ We have three more attributes of God to discuss, but if this were all we knew about Him, who could have a relationship with God? **Nobody**!

Allow this to sink in and you will see the person's countenance fall. The reason some people don't get excited about the good news is that they don't know about "the bad news." When we get "the bad news" on the table, the good news seems very good! Deal thoroughly with "the bad news" and he will be ready to receive God's exchange when you show it to him.

You should be able to deal with the first two points in less than ten minutes and still be thorough. It is not necessary to elaborate. The entire gospel presentation can be given in twenty minutes when necessary. If your friend participates in a back-and-forth conversation, it will take longer. Generally you will find a longer back-and-forth conversation is much more effective.

LESSON 6

ASSIGNMENT SHEET

- ☐ Complete the On the Job Training Debriefing Chart for last week's encounters.
- ☐ Pray with your prayer partners.
- ☐ Read Lesson 6, "God Is Just and cannot overlook our sin."
- ☐ Read chapters 16–18 from *Just What the Doctor Ordered.*
- ☐ Memorize John 1:14 and 1 Peter 3:18.
- ☐ Memorize Lesson 6 Memory Sheet.
- ☐ Say Lesson 6 Memory Sheet out loud from memory in front of a mirror.
- ☐ Say Lesson 6 Memory Sheet to someone before class.
- ☐ Have him check the points you remember, listening for accuracy.
- ☐ Hand out five gospel tracts.
- ☐ Pray for the lost and for God's power on your life.
- ☐ Evaluate your Find Five List, continue to actively pursue reaching the people on it, and add new people as needed.

LESSON 6

ONE-PAGE **MEMORY SHEET**

*"Come and see the works of God. . . . I will declare what he hath done for my soul." (Psalm 66:5*a*, 16*b*)*

☐ CONVERSATION

I must turn the conversation to the theme of themes.

- ☐ ① **Making Conversation**
- ☐ ② **Directing Conversation**
- ☐ "How would you describe your relationship with God?"
- ☐ "What do you think it takes to have a relationship with God and live with Him forever in heaven?"
- ☐ Personal Testimony—He has changed my life.
- ☐ "Are you 100% sure that all your sins are forgiven and you will go to heaven?"
- ☐ 1 John 5:13 or Titus 3:5
- ☐ "May I show you from the Bible how to have a relationship with God?"

☐ INTRODUCTION

I must introduce the sinner to the Savior.

- ☐ ① **God Is Holy** and cannot tolerate our sin.
  - ☐ **God's Intolerance**—Habakkuk 1:13*a*
  - ☐ **God's Reflection**—1 John 3:4*b*
    - Ten Commandments
  - ☐ **Man's Dilemma**—Romans 3:23
    - ☐ Illustration—Flagpole

- ☐ ② **God Is Just** and cannot overlook our sin.
  - ☐ **God's Standard**—Romans 6:23*a*
  - ☐ **God's Judgment**—Matthew 25:41
  - ☐ **Man's Destiny**—Revelation 21:8
    - ☐ Illustration—Judge acquitting a proven murderer/brother
    - "Would that be justice?"

- ☐ ③ **God Is Loving** and has reached out to us.
- ☐ He has provided a way for us to be close to Him that satisfies His holy/just nature (John 3:16).
  - ☐ **God's Son**
    - ☐ "Who would you say Jesus is?"
    - God in flesh—John 1:14
  - ☐ **God's Exchange**—Jesus becomes
    - ☐ Our Substitute—1 Peter 3:18
    - ☐ Our Righteousness—2 Corinthians 5:21
      - ☐ Illustration—My record/His record chart
    - ☐ Our Full Payment—1 John 1:7*b*; John 19:30
  - ☐ **Man's Deliverance** from sin and its penalty —1 Corinthians 15:3–4

- ☐ ④ **God Is Gracious** and offers salvation as a gift.
  - ☐ **God's Gift**—Ephesians 2:8–9
  - ☐ **God's Offer**—John 1:12
  - ☐ **Man's Decision**
    - ☐ Believe—Acts 16:31
      - ☐ Illustration—Blondine
      - Get in the wheelbarrow.

☐ INVITATION

I must offer the inquirer the gift of eternal life.

☐ ASSIMILATION

I must call the disciple to the life of Christ.

LESSON 6

GOD IS JUST AND CANNOT OVERLOOK OUR SIN

TOSSING THE PRESENTATION

At this point, the trainer can involve his trainee in the gospel presentation by utilizing these "Tossing the Presentation" Tools.

★ The first few attempts at participating in the presentation can be difficult. The trainer should plan to get into the presentation and then calmly say, "________ (trainee's name) has been studying God's holiness. ________ (trainee's name) why don't you tell ________ (friend's name) what you have learned?

★ When the trainee has gone as far as he can, teach him to simply ask, "________ (trainer's name) do you have anything you would like to add to that?" While this may be code for "Help" your new friend hears only that you have finished what you had studied.

from the One-Page Memory Sheet

☐ ② **God Is Just** and cannot overlook our sin.
God is called *"the Holy One and the Just" (Acts 3:14*b*)*
☐ **God's Standard**—Romans 6:23*a*
☐ **God's Judgment**—Matthew 25:41
☐ **Man's Destiny**—Revelation 21:8
☐ Illustration—Judge acquitting a proven murderer/brother
Would that be justice?

EXTRA VERSES THAT MIGHT BE HELPFUL

Deuteronomy 32:4—He is the Rock, his work is ***perfect****: for all his ways are* ***judgment****: a God of* ***truth*** *and* ***without iniquity****,* ***just*** *and* ***right*** *is he.*

He is the perfect, unchanging God, Whose every action is just. His very character is truth without any error, and He is always **just and right**. Remember He is perfect. He doesn't make any mistakes or commit any wrongs!

Hebrews 13:8—Jesus Christ ***the same yesterday, and to day, and for ever****.*

Because He doesn't change, His standard doesn't change from person to person.

*Acts 10:34*b—*God is no respecter of persons.*

*Psalm 111:7—**The works of his hands are verity [truth] and judgment [justice]**; all his commandments are sure.*

POSSIBLE TRANSITION STATEMENT

★ This is the bad news. We'll get to the good news in just a bit, but the bad news gets worse before it gets better. God not only is holy and cannot tolerate our sin but also is just and cannot overlook our sin. As the just God of all the earth, He must judge all of us by the same standard. "God is no respecter of persons" (Acts 10:34*b*). If this is true, and it is, then we need to know what His standard is.

I. God's standard

*Romans 6:23*a—*The wages of sin is death.*

A. Wages are the payment we deserve.

★ **Making It Real**
How often do you get paid?
You earned that, didn't you?
You deserve that, don't you?
What would you think if payday rolled around and you didn't get paid?
That wouldn't be fair. It's not just.

B. God's standard demands that sin receive the death penalty.

★ You may be thinking, "Wait a minute, even people who go to heaven die physically. What does it mean that 'the wages of sin are death'?" When Jesus told His disciples about the end times, He talked about the final judgment. Let's look at the scene He described.

II. God's judgment

Matthew 25:41—Then shall he say also unto them on the left hand, Depart from me, ye cursed, into everlasting fire, prepared for the devil and his angels.

A. God never intended for people to go to hell. He prepared this eternal place of judgment for the Devil and his angels.

B. Yet, this verse describes people being cast into judgment!

★ If I were you, I would want to know who those people are. The last book of the Bible is called the Revelation. In it God reveals what is going to happen to mankind, and He gives us a list of the people who are condemned.

EXTRA VERSES THAT MIGHT BE HELPFUL

Some may take exception to teaching that God would send anyone to hell. Show them what He has revealed to us about Himself in His Word.

Hebrews 9:27—And as it is appointed unto men once to die, but after this the judgment.

Psalm 89:14—Justice and judgment are the habitation [environment] of thy throne: mercy and truth shall go before thy face.

Psalm 9:7–8—But the Lord shall endure for ever: he hath prepared his throne for judgment. And he shall judge the world in righteousness, he shall minister judgment to the people in uprightness.

Ezekiel 18:20—The soul that sinneth, it shall die. The son shall not bear the iniquity of the father, neither shall the father bear the iniquity of the son: the righteousness of the righteous shall be upon him, and the wickedness of the wicked shall be upon him.

Revelation 20:11–15—And I saw a great white throne, and him that sat on it, from whose face the earth and the heaven fled away; and there was found no place for them. And I saw the dead, small and great, stand before God; and the books were opened: and another book was opened, which is the book of life: and the dead were judged out of those things which were written in the books, according to their works. And the sea gave up the dead which were in it; and death and hell delivered up the dead which were in them: and they were judged every man according to their works. And death and hell were cast into the lake of fire. This is the second death. And whosoever was not found written in the book of life was cast into the lake of fire.

C. **The Real Question**

"If we were holy, we'd realize that the strange thing isn't why God would send people to hell. The real disturbing question (if we were holy) would be, 'How could a holy God send sinful men to heaven?' We ask the wrong question because we don't grasp the truth. Therefore we don't grasp the wonders of grace.

"We imagine that hell is out of proportion to our offenses precisely because we don't grasp how serious they are. God's grace faces hell's reality straight on, offering full deliverance. Denying hell takes the wind out of grace's sails."

Randy Alcorn, *The Grace and Truth Paradox* (Sisters, Oregon: Multnomah, 2003), 75.

Note: Twenty-nine percent of people in America who identified themselves as non-Christian said they think they will go to heaven.

Two percent of non-Christians said they think they will go to hell and 5 percent of non-Christians said they think they will go to purgatory.

Thirty-two percent of non-Christians said they think they will go somewhere else.

Thirty-three percent of non-Christians don't know.

USA Today Snapshot, April 17, 2003

Somehow even today there is an awareness of the afterlife, and God uses His Word to fully convince men of this truth.

III. Man's destiny

Revelation 21:8—But the fearful, and unbelieving, and the abominable, and murderers, and whoremongers, and sorcerers, and idolaters, and ***all liars, shall have their part in the lake which burns with fire and brimstone****: which is the second death.*

★ When we sin, we alienate ourselves from God because of His holy nature. His just nature demands that He judge each of us for our own personal sins.

A. These definitions of sin are very convicting.

fearful—those who are afraid to trust the Lord (Maybe they're afraid of what their family or friends might say.)

unbelieving—those who don't believe the Bible

abominable—those who are sexually perverse

murderers—those who unlawfully, premeditatedly take a life

whoremongers—those who indulge in sex outside of marriage (This word is most often translated *fornicators* in the Bible. The English word *pornography* comes from this Greek word.)

sorcerers—includes those who use drugs, those involved in the occult, or witchcraft (The English word *pharmaceuticals* comes from this Greek word.)

idolaters—those who place anything in their lives as more important than God

all liars—those who tell a lie (A lie can be everything from a "whopper" to stretching the truth.)

POSSIBLE TRANSITION STATEMENT

★ That's a pretty rough list. No doubt you probably haven't done most of the things on the list, but you and I both have admitted that we have lied. How many murders does a man have to commit before we consider him to be a murderer? Only one! How many lies does a person have to tell before God considers him a liar? Only one! The Bible tells us that all liars are going to be condemned to hell! In fact, the wages of all sin, big and little, are death in hell, separated from God forever.

EXTRA VERSES THAT MIGHT BE HELPFUL

Revelation 20:14–15—And death and hell were cast into the lake of fire. This is the second death. And whosoever was not found written in the book of life was cast into the lake of fire.

Matthew 25:46—And these shall go away into ***everlasting punishment****: but the righteous into life eternal.*

*Mark 9:45*b*–46—It is better for thee to enter halt into life, than having two feet to be cast into hell, into the fire that never shall be quenched: where their worm dieth not, and the fire is not quenched.*

Luke 16:19–24—There was a certain rich man. . . . and in hell he lift up his eyes, ***being in torments****, and seeth Abraham afar off, and Lazarus in his bosom. And he cried and said, Father Abraham, have mercy on me, and send Lazarus, that he may dip the tip of his finger in water, and cool my tongue; for I am tormented in this flame.*

1. **Be clear**. Our flesh tempts us to back off of this point. Again, let the Holy Spirit use His sword to convince the sinner of the truth that he is under condemnation.

   *John 3:18*a*—He that believeth on him is not condemned: but* ***he that believeth not is condemned already****.*

   Repentance comes from dealing with sin and judgment sufficiently. Don't let up here. It will pay dividends later!

   #### MAN IN THE PARK

   I was in a park in the Philippines and began witnessing to two college-aged men. One of them boldly proclaimed that he didn't believe in hell. I responded by telling him that if he told me he didn't believe there was a Denver, Colorado, it wouldn't matter to me, because I had been to Denver. I knew it was there. Continuing, I told him his not believing there was a hell didn't make it any less real. Hell is real, and we must all prepare for eternity so that we don't go there. He left convinced of his need to avoid hell and promised to think about it more.

   Note: Unshakable, personal convincement is often one of the best arguments.

2. **Be compassionate**. We need to share this truth with our own heart broken. The truth about hell

needs no drama to give it a sobering effect. If your friend is following you at all, he will be devastated to think that he is headed for hell.

B. No one can have an accurate understanding of God without understanding His just nature.

1. If your friend does not understand, keep teaching until he does.

2. If he denies the truth of God's judgment, keep going. Give the Bible a chance to do its work to convince him! Remember, the good news is about Jesus' payment. **Don't quit before you get to the exchange**.

3. Some soulwinners don't like this point. While our flesh does not like confrontation, the Spirit is working in the world to convict the sinner of judgment. We must yield to the Spirit's plan and speak the truth in love.

C. Your friend might say, "That's not fair."

1. There is a difference between justice and fairness.

a. Fairness is most often determined by feelings.

b. Justice is determined by facts.

Most of the people who are in prison are there justly. They broke some law of the land and were held accountable to that law. They may not feel that they have been treated fairly, but that does not change the fact that justice has been served.

2. Justice is not defined by what we feel or want but by fixed laws or facts.

One definition for justice is "the administration . . . of law."

D. Just as God is holy and cannot tolerate sin; He is also just and cannot ignore sin.

POSSIBLE TRANSITION STATEMENT

★ You might be saying, "I thought God was a loving God. How can He judge men like that?"

ILLUSTRATION

Judge acquitting a proven murderer: Imagine a judge presiding over a murder trial. There is a mountain of evidence to prove that the defendant is guilty. Would justice be served if the judge chose to overlook obvious guilt and acquit the murderer? No! What if the guilty man were the judge's brother, and he loved him very much and chose to overlook his guilt and acquit him? Would that be justice? No! His love for the guilty would not change the demand for justice!

LESSON 7

ASSIGNMENT SHEET

- ☐ Complete the On the Job Training Debriefing Chart for last week's encounters.
- ☐ Pray with your prayer partners.
- ☐ Read Lesson 7, "God Is Loving and has reached out to us."
- ☐ Read chapters 19–21 from *Just What the Doctor Ordered.*
- ☐ Memorize 2 Corinthians 5:21 and 1 John 1:7*b.*
- ☐ Memorize Lesson 7 Memory Sheet.
- ☐ Say Lesson 7 Memory Sheet out loud from memory in front of a mirror.
- ☐ Say Lesson 7 Memory Sheet to someone before class.
  Have him check the points you remember, listening for accuracy.
- ☐ Hand out five gospel tracts.
- ☐ Pray for the lost and for God's power on your life.
- ☐ Evaluate your Find Five List, continue to actively pursue reaching the people on it, and add new people as needed.

LESSON 7

ONE-PAGE **MEMORY SHEET**

"Come and see the works of God. . . . I will declare what he hath done for my soul." (Psalm 66:5a, 16b)

☐ **CONVERSATION**
I must turn the conversation to the theme of themes.

☐ ① **Making Conversation**
☐ ② **Directing Conversation**
☐ "How would you describe your relationship with God?"
☐ "What do you think it takes to have a relationship with God and live with Him forever in heaven?"
☐ Personal Testimony—He has changed my life.
☐ "Are you 100% sure that all your sins are forgiven and you will go to heaven?"
☐ 1 John 5:13 or Titus 3:5
☐ "May I show you from the Bible how to have a relationship with God?"

☐ **INTRODUCTION**
I must introduce the sinner to the Savior.

☐ ① **God Is Holy** and cannot tolerate our sin.
☐ **God's Intolerance**—Habakkuk 1:13*a*
☐ **God's Reflection**—1 John 3:4*b*
Ten Commandments
☐ **Man's Dilemma**—Romans 3:23
☐ Illustration—Flagpole

☐ ② **God Is Just** and cannot overlook our sin.
☐ **God's Standard**—Romans 6:23*a*
☐ **God's Judgment**—Matthew 25:41
☐ **Man's Destiny**—Revelation 21:8
☐ Illustration—Judge acquitting a proven murderer/brother
"Would that be justice?"

☐ ③ **God Is Loving** and has reached out to us.
☐ He has provided a way for us to be close to Him that satisfies His holy/just nature (John 3:16).
☐ **God's Son**
☐ "Who would you say Jesus is?"
God in flesh—John 1:14
☐ **God's Exchange**—Jesus becomes
☐ Our Substitute—1 Peter 3:18
☐ Our Righteousness—2 Corinthians 5:21
☐ Illustration—My record/His record chart
☐ Our Full Payment—1 John 1:7*b*; John 19:30
☐ **Man's Deliverance** from sin and its penalty —1 Corinthians 15:3–4

☐ ④ **God Is Gracious** and offers salvation as a gift.
☐ **God's Gift**—Ephesians 2:8–9
☐ **God's Offer**—John 1:12
☐ **Man's Decision**
☐ Believe—Acts 16:31
☐ Illustration—Blondine
Get in the wheelbarrow.

The Three Elements of Saving Faith

Understand
God can't tolerate or overlook my sin. He gave His life in exchange for mine and wants to give me eternal life.

Agree
I am a sinner and need a Savior.

Depend/Trust
I choose to receive Jesus' exchange—my sin and its penalty for His record and eternal life.

☐ Illustration—Two chairs
☐ Transfer dependence/trust
☐ Repent—Luke 13:5, change of mind
☐ Illustration—Point of no return
What would you do?

☐ **INVITATION**
I must offer the inquirer the gift of eternal life.

☐ **ASSIMILATION**
I must call the disciple to the life of Christ.

LESSON 7

GOD IS LOVING AND HAS REACHED OUT TO US

from the One-Page Memory Sheet

- ☐ ③ **God Is Loving** and has reached out to u**s**.
- ☐ He has provided a way for us to be close to Him that satisfies His holy/just nature.
  John 3:16—For God so loved the world, that He gave His only begotten Son, that whosoever believeth in Him should not perish, but have everlasting life.
- ☐ **God's Son**
- ☐ "Who would you say Jesus is?"
- ☐ God in flesh—John 1:14
- ☐ **God's Exchange**—Jesus becomes:
- ☐ Our Substitute—1 Peter 3:18
- ☐ Our Righteousness—2 Corinthians 5:21
- ☐ Illustration—My record/His record chart
- ☐ Our Full Payment—1 John 1:7*b*; John 19:30
- ☐ **Man's Deliverance** from sin and its penalty—1 Corinthians 15:3–4

POSSIBLE TRANSITION STATEMENT

★ God is holy and cannot tolerate our sin and just so that He cannot overlook our sin. God is loving and has reached out to us; but even in His love, He cannot do anything that will violate the rest of His nature. Through the gift of Jesus He provided a way for us to be close to Him that satisfies His holy, just nature.

★ When the Bible states, "God so loved the world," it means every man and woman in the world. To get to know Him, it is imperative to know that **He loves you personally!**

EXTRA VERSES THAT MIGHT BE HELPFUL

*1 John 4:8*b—***God is love***.

Jeremiah 31:3—The Lord hath appeared of old unto me, saying, Yea, ***I have loved thee with an everlasting love: therefore with lovingkindness have I drawn thee***.

Matthew 11:19 —Jesus was called *"**a friend of . . . sinners**."*

Romans 5:8—But ***God*** *commendeth* ***[stretched forth] his love toward us****, in that,* ***while we were yet sinners****, Christ died for us.*

★ A good way to teach this is to begin with the question "Who would you say Jesus is?"

I. God's Son

John 1:14—And the Word [Jesus] was made flesh, and dwelt among us, (and we beheld his glory, the glory as of the only begotten of the Father,) full of grace and truth.

A. It is necessary to be clear with this point.

Jesus is God in the flesh. As such, He was uniquely qualified to pay our sin penalty.

1. Your friend may answer, "The son of God."

   A good way to help him recognize the fullness of Jesus' deity is to ask, "In one respect I am a son of God because I have received Him as my Savior. Would you say that Jesus is different from me?"

   Most of the time this brings a bit of levity, and you can proceed to teach your friend why Jesus is very different from you.

2. Your friend may answer, "A good man" or "A great teacher."

   Remember he asked you to show him from the Bible how to have a relationship with God. Don't argue. At this point you don't need to convince him. Just show him what the Bible teaches and give the Holy Spirit a chance to convince him.

   EXTRA VERSES THAT MIGHT BE HELPFUL

   Matthew 1:23—Behold, a virgin shall be with child, and shall bring forth a son, and they shall call his name Emmanuel, which being interpreted is, God with us.

   Philippians 2:5b–8—Christ Jesus: who, being in the form of God, thought it not robbery to be equal with God: but made himself of no reputation, and took upon him the form of a servant, and was made in the likeness of men: and being found in fashion as a man, he humbled himself, and became obedient unto death, even the death of the cross.

   If your friend is having a hard time accepting that Jesus is God come down to earth in a human body, the argument that Jesus claimed to be equal with God is a powerful argument.

   "I and my Father are one. Then the Jews took up stones again to stone him." (John 10:30–31)

   In *Mere Christianity*, C. S. Lewis used the argument that Jesus was either genuinely **Lord**, a **liar**, or a **lunatic**. He was either telling the truth and really was God in the flesh, or He was only a deceiver acting the part. If that were the case, we cannot call Him a good man. The only other option is that He was deceived Himself and thought He was God, but wasn't. If that were the case, we cannot call Him a great teacher.

B. Other truths about Jesus that must be clear

It is not necessary for your friend to know everything you know about Jesus, but it is important that he believe everything he does know.

Philip had been a follower of Jesus only a few days when he began introducing others to Christ. There is no way of knowing what Philip did or did not know at this point. He may have known about the virgin birth, but he certainly wasn't very careful about how he described Jesus.

John 1:45—Philip findeth Nathanael, and saith unto him, We have found him, of whom Moses in the law, and the prophets, did write, Jesus of Nazareth, ***the son of Joseph****.*

1. Jesus was born of a virgin.

   Matthew 1:23—Behold, a virgin shall be with child, and shall bring forth a son, and they shall call his name Emmanuel, which being interpreted is, God with us.

2. Jesus lived a sinless life.

   *Hebrews 4:15*b —Jesus "was in all points tempted like as we are, **yet without sin**."

3. There is only one God.

   *Deuteronomy 6:4*b—*The Lord our God* ***is one Lord****.*

4. Jesus is the only mediator.

   1 Timothy 2:5—For ***there is one God****, and one mediator between God and men, the man Christ Jesus.*

5. Jesus is the only way to an intimate relationship with God.

   John 14:6—Jesus saith unto him, I am the way, the truth, and the life: no man cometh unto the Father, but by me.

II. God's exchange

★ Though He is God in heaven, He humbled Himself and became a man so that He could give His life in exchange for all men, who have sinned.

A. **Our substitute**—Jesus has given Himself as our substitute.

   *1 Peter 3:18*a—*For Christ also hath once suffered for sins, the* ***just for the unjust****, that he might bring us to God.*

1. As the holy/just God Who came in human form, He is the only One qualified to die in our place.

2. Notice the exchange—**the just for the unjust**.

3. He took our sins on Himself when He died on the cross.

   EXTRA VERSES THAT MIGHT BE HELPFUL

   1 Peter 2:24—Who his own self bare our sins in his own body on the tree, that we, being dead to sins, should live unto righteousness: by whose stripes ye were healed.

   *Isaiah 53:10*a—*Yet it pleased the Lord to bruise him; he hath put him to grief: when thou shalt make his soul an offering for sin.*

   1 John 4:10—Herein is love, not that we loved God, but that he loved us, and sent his Son to be the propitiation for our sins.

   As our substitute, Jesus bore the wrath of our sin. God's demand for justice has been satisfied.

   2 Corinthians 8:9—For ye know the grace of our Lord Jesus Christ, that, though he was rich, yet for your sakes he became poor, that ye through his poverty might be rich.

   This is a great verse to demonstrate Jesus' trading places with us in the exchange He offers.

B. **Our righteousness**—God has offered us His perfect righteousness.

2 Corinthians 5:21—For he [God] hath made him [Jesus] to be sin for us, who knew no sin; ***that we might be made the righteousness of God in him****.*

1. Jesus dealt with your sinful record thoroughly, but He also offers His own record as a perfect completion to the exchange.

2. When we receive His offer, we take His righteous record and meet His holy standard.

3. Now God can give us a home with Him in heaven forever and still be just.

ILLUSTRATION

My Record/His Record Chart

Ask your friend if you can make a record of some of the offenses for which God will judge him. You might want to add,
★ "I don't know about you, but mine would fill up a huge book."

Giving the Exchange Gospel Presentation System (GPS) has an exchange chart already filled out. The GPS is a four-page, full-color flip chart for the *Giving the Exchange* Gospel Presentation. It keeps you from getting lost while giving the gospel. You can find it at www.exchangemessage.org.

Jesus'	**John Doe's**
~~John Doe's~~ Record	~~Jesus'~~ Record
Lying	Holy
Coveting	Just
Stealing	Accepted by God
	Free to live with God

Put your friend's name at the top of the list. You can write: lying, cheating, hating, coveting, disrespect, and so forth. Now make another column and put Jesus' name at the top.

★ What is His record before God?
You could write: holy, just, Son of God, accepted by God, free to live with God, and so forth.

★ Second Corinthians 5:21 teaches that God put all your sins on Jesus when He died.
Cross out your friend's name and write Jesus.

★ That takes care of your record, but that is not all God wants to do. The verse continues, "that we might be made the righteousness of God in Him."

Now cross out Jesus' name and write your friend's name.

4. This is the reality of the exchange Jesus offers us!

   a. He suffered as a lying, coveting thief in our place.

   b. He offers us the ability to have a full relationship with God as our Father, accepted by Him because of Jesus' holy, just nature.

C. **Our full payment**

1 John 1:7b—The blood of Jesus Christ his Son cleanseth us from all sin.

1. Someone may still think, "I see that, but surely I must do something!"

   Ask this question, "Can this mean all the sins I have ever committed?"

   It says **all**! Of course it means all your sins.

   (You can determine what your friend is thinking by asking questions.)

2. Another may think, "Yes, but I still have to keep myself from sinning to stay forgiven. It can't mean my future sins."

   Tell this person to consider that all our sins were future when Jesus died. He forgave all our sins—past, present, and even future!

3. One of the last things Jesus said before He died is recorded in John 19:30. "He said, **It is finished**."

   a. The word in the original language is *tetelestai* and means "paid in full."

   b. If He paid the entire price, then what is left for you to pay? Nothing!

      Caution: Be careful how you ask this question. Your saying, "Is there anything left for you to do?" can be confusing. There is something left to do. He has to actually make the exchange with Jesus. Asking if there is anything left to pay makes it clear that Jesus paid it all.

      KARLTON
      Karlton had been a scoffer but was willing to do *The Exchange* Bible study. He had heard the entire gospel presentation the first time we met together. After only two lessons he responded to a public invitation in the morning service at our church. His words were classic. "Pastor, I don't need to study anymore; I know it's true. I want to make that exchange with Jesus."

III. Man's deliverance

*1Corinthians 15:3b–4—Christ died for our sins . . . and . . . **rose again the third day**.*

A. Jesus became a man and experienced death for us so that He could defeat death and set us free from its power. When He rose from the grave, Jesus proved that He was indeed powerful enough to win the victory over sin and its penalty, death and hell.

*1 Corinthians 15:5–8—And that **he was seen** of Cephas, then of the twelve: after that, **he was seen** of above five hundred brethren at once; of whom the greater part remain unto this present, but some are fallen asleep. After that, **he was seen** of James; then of all the apostles. And last of all **he was seen** of me also, as of one born out of due time.*

1. In my Bible I have underlined the phrase "He was seen."

2. It is not always necessary to turn there, but when you need to, it is very powerful just to show the volume of witnesses.

3. The resurrection is one of the best-proved events of history.

4. When necessary, it is also valuable to point out the change in the disciples who were listed as

eyewitnesses. They went from hiding after Christ's death to a boldness that led all but one of them to martyrdom. What was different? In addition to receiving the Holy Spirit, these men had seen the risen Savior. They knew He had risen, they had seen Him, and they gave their lives telling others about Him.

B. His resurrection also proved that God was satisfied with His payment for our sins.

When the priest went into the holy of holies, the high priest had to perfectly follow the law before God could accept his offering. The proof that God had accepted the offering was that the priest came out from behind the veil alive. When Jesus returned from the grave alive, He proved that God had accepted His payment for your sins and mine.

POSSIBLE TRANSITION STATEMENT

★ God loves much more than most people suspect, and His love is powerful enough to reach even sinners like you and me!

LESSON 8

ASSIGNMENT SHEET

- ☐ Complete the On the Job Training Debriefing Chart for last week's encounters.
- ☐ Pray with your prayer partners.
- ☐ Read Lesson 8, "God Is Gracious and offers salvation as a gift."
- ☐ Read chapters 22–24 from *Just What the Doctor Ordered.*
- ☐ Memorize John 19:30*b* and 1 Corinthians 15:3–4.
- ☐ Memorize Lesson 8 Memory Sheet.
- ☐ Say Lesson 8 Memory Sheet out loud from memory in front of a mirror.
- ☐ Say Lesson 8 Memory Sheet to someone before class.
  Have him check the points you remember, listening for accuracy.
- ☐ Hand out five gospel tracts.
- ☐ Pray for the lost and for God's power on your life.
- ☐ Evaluate your Find Five List, continue to actively pursue reaching the people on it, and add new people as needed.

LESSON 8

ONE-PAGE **MEMORY SHEET**

*"Come and see the works of God. . . . I will declare what he hath done for my soul." (Psalm 66:5*a*, 16*b*)*

☐ **CONVERSATION**
I must turn the conversation to the theme of themes.

☐ ① **Making Conversation**
☐ ② **Directing Conversation**
☐ "How would you describe your relationship with God?"
☐ "What do you think it takes to have a relationship with God and live with Him forever in heaven?"
☐ Personal Testimony—He has changed my life.
☐ "Are you 100% sure that all your sins are forgiven and you will go to heaven?"
☐ 1 John 5:13 or Titus 3:5
☐ "May I show you from the Bible how to have a relationship with God?"

☐ **INTRODUCTION**
I must introduce the sinner to the Savior.

☐ ① **God Is Holy** and cannot tolerate our sin.
☐ **God's Intolerance**—Habakkuk 1:13*a*
☐ **God's Reflection**—1 John 3:4*b*
Ten Commandments
☐ **Man's Dilemma**—Romans 3:23
☐ Illustration—Flagpole

☐ ② **God Is Just** and cannot overlook our sin.
☐ **God's Standard**—Romans 6:23*a*
☐ **God's Judgment**—Matthew 25:41
☐ **Man's Destiny**—Revelation 21:8
☐ Illustration—Judge acquitting a proven murderer/brother
"Would that be justice?"

☐ ③ **God Is Loving** and has reached out to us.
☐ He has provided a way for us to be close to Him that satisfies His holy/just nature (John 3:16).
☐ **God's Son**
☐ "Who would you say Jesus is?"
God in flesh—John 1:14
☐ **God's Exchange**—Jesus becomes
☐ Our Substitute—1 Peter 3:18
☐ Our Righteousness—2 Corinthians 5:21
☐ Illustration—My record/His record chart
☐ Our Full Payment—1 John 1:7*b*; John 19:30
☐ **Man's Deliverance** from sin and its penalty —1 Corinthians 15:3–4

☐ ④ **God Is Gracious** and offers salvation as a gift.
☐ **God's Gift**—Ephesians 2:8–9
☐ **God's Offer**—John 1:12
☐ **Man's Decision**
☐ Believe—Acts 16:31
☐ Illustration—Blondine
Get in the wheelbarrow.

The Three Elements of Saving Faith

Understand
God can't tolerate or overlook my sin. He gave His life in exchange for mine and wants to give me eternal life.

Agree
I am a sinner and need a Savior.

Depend/Trust
I choose to receive Jesus' exchange—my sin and its penalty for His record and eternal life.

☐ Illustration—Two chairs
☐ Transfer dependence/trust
☐ Repent—Luke 13:5, change of mind
☐ Illustration—Point of no return
What would you do?

☐ **INVITATION**
I must offer the inquirer the gift of eternal life.

☐ ① **Ask**
☐ "Do you believe that Jesus loves you and will give you forgiveness and eternal life if you ask Him?"
☐ "Then are you willing to receive Him right now?"
☐ ② **Pray**
☐ ③ **Welcome**

☐ **ASSIMILATION**
I must call the disciple to the life of Christ.

LESSON 8

GOD IS GRACIOUS AND OFFERS SALVATION AS A GIFT

from the One-Page Memory Sheet

☐ ④ **God Is Gracious** and offers salvation as a gift.
Psalm 116:5—Gracious is the Lord, and righteous; yea, our God is merciful.
☐ **God's Gift**—Ephesians 2:8–9
☐ **God's Offer**—John 1:12
☐ **Man's Decision**
☐ Believe—Acts 16:31
☐ Illustration—Blondine
Get in the wheelbarrow.

The Three Elements of Saving Faith

Understand
God can't tolerate or overlook my sin. He gave His life in exchange for mine and wants to give me eternal life.

Agree
I am a sinner and need a Savior.

Depend/Trust
I choose to receive Jesus' exchange—my sin and its penalty for His record and eternal life.

☐ Illustration—Two chairs
☐ Transfer dependence/trust
☐ Repent—Luke 13:5, change of mind
☐ Illustration—Point of no return
What would you do?

POSSIBLE TRANSITION STATEMENT

★ Just as the bad news of our sin and its penalty got worse before it got better, the good news of God's love gets better as we go. God is gracious and gives salvation as a gift. This is exhilarating and humbling at the same time. It means that salvation is within my grasp, but it also means that I don't have the ability to do **anything** to earn it.

The key thought is that Christ's exchange **cannot be purchased** and must be received as a gift by faith **plus nothing**.

★ **Grace** is God giving me what I do not deserve. **Mercy** is God not giving me what I do deserve. These definitions are helpful but simplistic. God's grace is His enabling me to do what I cannot do without Him. God's mercy is often expressed by His giving me what I do deserve so that I will turn from my self and my sin to Him.

Grace has been explained this way:

GOD'S **R**ICHES **A**T **C**HRIST'S **E**XPENSE

I. God's gift

Ephesians 2:8–9—For ***by grace*** *are ye saved through faith; and that not of yourselves:* ***it is the gift of God: not of works****, lest any man should boast.*

A. Grace is God's giving to us what we can never earn for ourselves.

B. Grace is not our earning part and God's giving us part. We don't have the ability to earn holiness or meet His just demands. It is as if God is saying, "Your money is no good here."

WOMAN AT AN EXCHANGE SEMINAR

A woman at one of our seminars told a story that illustrates this point. She was a widow with two small children. Money was tight, but her tires were badly worn and had to be replaced. She had new tires put on her car and when she tried to pay, the manager told her that someone had already paid for her tires. She couldn't pay for the tires because she didn't have the money and they had already been paid for. That is exactly where we are with God. Not only can we never pay the debt we owe, but Jesus paid it for us.

C. God's grace is enough.

*Romans 5:20*b*—Where sin abounded,* ***grace*** *did much more* ***abound****.*

1. Your friend may be feeling as though his sin is too bad or too much.

2. Many times the problem is that he has tried to quit sinning and has failed.

   Be careful how you deal with this issue. If you're not careful, you will communicate **grace plus works**. Giving up his sin does not save a person! Accepting the finished work of Christ on the cross saves him.

   It is important to recognize that **sin is the problem** that causes judgment, but **ceasing to sin is not the solution**. Receiving the finished work of Jesus on the cross is the solution. Many times confusion can be alleviated by teaching him the following concept:

   ★ God is interested in helping you to stop sinning, but that is not your main problem. Even if you were able to stop sinning, that wouldn't fix your relationship with God. You need God's gift of grace!

3. The issue to deal with is the sufficiency of God's grace. It doesn't matter how big the sin is or how hard it is to quit. What matters is that **God does the saving** and that He is powerful enough to deal with any sin.

EXTRA VERSES THAT MIGHT BE HELPFUL

Titus 3:5—Not by works of righteousness which we have done, but according to his mercy he saved us, by the washing of regeneration, and renewing of the Holy Ghost.

*Romans 4:4–5, 16*a*—Now to him that worketh is the reward not reckoned of grace, but of debt. But to him that worketh not, but believeth on him that justifieth the ungodly, his faith is counted for righteousness. . . . Therefore it is of faith, that it might be by grace.*

Romans 11:6—And if by grace, then is it no more of works: otherwise grace is no more grace. But if it be of works, then is it no more grace: otherwise work is no more work.

Romans 3:28—Therefore we conclude that a man is justified by faith without the deeds of the law.

II. God's offer

*John 1:12—But **as many as received him**, to them gave he power to become the sons of God, even to them that believe on his name.*

So if He does all the giving, what do we do? **Receive**. He offers to exchange His record for ours as a gift! All we can do is receive it.

Making It Real
If your friend doesn't seem to understand try this:

Hold out an object (a pen or pencil) in your hand, close enough for your friend to reach.

★ Ask, "If I told you that I wanted to give this to you, what would you have to do to get it?"

Keep holding it there. Eventually it will get awkward and he will either have to take it or say "Take it" or do both.

Sometimes you have to give him the answer, but the object lesson is much more effective if he comes up with the answer on his own.

POSSIBLE TRANSITION STATEMENT

★ So, how do we receive God's gift of salvation? Notice the last part of the verse: "even to them that believe on his name."

III. Man's decision

A. Believe

When the early disciples were asked, "What must I do to be saved?" (Acts 16:30), they simply answered "Believe on the Lord Jesus Christ, and thou shalt be saved" (Acts 16:31).

★ If the most important issue in your life depends on one simple word—*believe*—then you better know how to define it.

1. **Common faith**—A common definition of faith is "to understand a fact and to agree with it" (common faith).

2. **Saving faith**—Saving faith includes those two parts of the definition (to understand and to agree) but adds a third, dependence. We must choose to depend, rely, or trust on Jesus to forgive our sins and give us His righteousness.

a.

> **The Three Elements of Saving Faith**
>
> **Understand**
> God can't tolerate or overlook my sin. He gave His life in exchange for mine and wants to give me eternal life.
>
> **Agree**
> I am a sinner and need a Savior.
>
> **Depend/Trust**
> I choose to receive Jesus' exchange—my sin and its penalty for His record and eternal life.

C. H. Spurgeon, *All of Grace* (Grand Rapids: Baker Book House, 1976) 44–49.

★ Here is a story that helps us understand this third element of saving faith.

ILLUSTRATION

In 1859, the famous acrobat Charles Blondine stretched a tightrope 190 feet above the waters of Niagara Falls. Crowds gathered daily as he navigated the thousand-foot span. He walked across in a large burlap bag. He carried his manager across on his back. He even fitted a special wheelbarrow for the rope and pushed it across. Once, he put a cookstove in the wheelbarrow and stopped in the middle of the rope to cook and eat an omelet. The story is told that once while working with the wheelbarrow, he approached the cheering crowd and asked them who *believed* (that's the word we want to define) he could put a man in the wheelbarrow and take him across. The crowd went wild. Everyone wanted to see that stunt. They began to chant, "I believe, I believe, I believe!"

Blondine pointed to a man waving his hand and chanting, "I believe, I believe!" He said to the man, "You, sir, get in the wheelbarrow."

The man bolted in the other direction. What was wrong? The man believed that Blondine could put a man, some other man, into the wheelbarrow, but he wasn't willing to place his dependence on Blondine to take him across.

That's the way it is with a lot of people. They believe that Jesus died to deal with sins, but they have never chosen to trust Him to forgive their sins.

WOMAN IN THE WHEELBARROW

Several years ago, before I wrote *The Exchange* Bible study, I was witnessing to a couple who had visited our church. I had given them the gospel and had used this illustration about Blondine. The man seemed uninterested, so I began to wrap up the conversation in preparation to leave. (Now I would invite them to do *The Exchange*, the four-lesson Bible study.) The woman could tell I was getting ready to leave and exclaimed, "Wait a minute! I want to get in the wheelbarrow."

b. Saving faith is choosing to trust Christ's payment for sin as your own payment and nothing else.

1) It's a transaction. Your friend must choose to trust in what Christ has already done for him on the cross.

2) It's an exchange. In exchange for your friend's sinful record, Jesus gives His righteousness record and eternal life.

When people state they wish they had more faith, they are revealing their belief that faith is something that happens to them rather than something they do. Faith is an act of the will, a choice.

★ Here's another story that will help clarify this point

ILLUSTRATION

Imagine two chairs sitting side by side. The one on the left represents you and your efforts to get to heaven on your own, and the one on the right represents the finished payment of Christ for all your sins. If you are sitting in the chair representing self, what do you have to do to transfer your dependence to the chair representing Christ? You have to get out of the one chair and sit in the other. To transfer your dependence to God's grace for salvation, you have to stop depending on what you can do.

It is a decision. Just like someone would have had to get in Blondine's wheelbarrow to demonstrate real dependence on his ability to take him across, even so you have to **decide** to trust Jesus alone to give you eternal life in heaven.

Can he split his trust? What if a person decided to sit in both chairs? Is he really trusting in either chair? No! When a person tries to trust in Jesus **and** his own efforts, he is really showing that he doubts that Jesus is enough.

POSSIBLE TRANSITION STATEMENT

★ Another word the Bible uses to describe this decision is *repent*.

B. Repent

Jesus said, "Except ye repent, ye shall all . . . perish" (Luke 13:5).

1. The word *repent* means "to change one's mind."

   a. If your friend has been thinking his sin isn't bad enough to keep him from heaven, **he'll have to change his mind about that**.

   b. If he has been thinking he can do enough good to counterbalance the bad things he has done, **he'll have to change his mind about that**.

   c. He cannot believe that he will make it to heaven by any other way but Jesus. All other thinking has to be abandoned.

   This portion of the outline is given to bring the discussion to a decision. A good way to help your friend come to a decision is to remind him what he said it takes to have a relationship with God.

   ★ "Earlier you said you thought your good works would be enough to get you to heaven. You're going to have to change your mind about that."

2. Repentance is a decision, not a feeling.

   a. Emotions often accompany repentance when a person realizes how wrong he has been.

   Caution: If a person is waiting for a feeling before he makes a decision, then he may be relying on an experience, not the Savior.

   b. The essence of repentance is to admit that **God is right** to condemn your sin and that **you have been wrong**.

   GOD, YOU ARE RIGHT. I AM WRONG.

   At the end of each lesson of *The Exchange* Bible study there is a question: "If you were going to talk to God about what you have learned in this Bible study, what would you tell Him?"

This is an actual prayer written by a man after finishing lesson 2.

> **Dear God,**
>
> **I am a sinner. I am guilty of adultery, lying, taking God's name in vain, envy, and greed. I deserve punishment in hell. You are right; I am wrong. You are just and I am deserving judgment. Please be merciful to me. I believe the truth of Jesus Christ.**
>
> **Amen.**

★ The reason we can be 100 percent sure we're on our way to heaven is because Jesus does 100 percent of the saving.

CLOSING ILLUSTRATION

There is a point of no return on the Niagara River, where the current from the falls is too powerful for a boat to navigate safely. It's marked clearly with warnings because if a boat goes past that point, it is bound to be pulled by the current over the roaring falls. Imagine a man in a rowboat absentmindedly crossing that line. When he realizes what he has done, he tries to turn back to safety, but it is too late. No matter how hard he rows, he is still being pulled inch by inch closer to impending doom. Suppose someone on the shore sees his plight and expertly throws a rope across his lap. **Now he has a choice to make**. Will he keep up his own efforts only to eventually plunge to sure destruction, or will he drop the oars of self-effort and trust the rope of safety? What would you do?

What does the Bible say is necessary to receive God's grace?

*James 4:6*b—***God** resisteth [fights against] the proud, but **giveth grace unto the humble**.*

- Your friend has to humble himself.
- He must admit that he has sinned and that his sin is an offense to our holy God.
- He must admit that he can't save himself from God's righteous judgment.
- He must choose to trust in the loving gift of Jesus' sacrifice to forgive his sins.

LESSON 9

ASSIGNMENT SHEET

- ☐ Complete the On the Job Training Debriefing Chart for last week's encounters.
- ☐ Pray with your prayer partners.
- ☐ Read Lesson 9, "Invitation."
- ☐ Read chapters 25–27 from *Just What the Doctor Ordered.*
- ☐ Memorize Ephesians 2:8–9 and John 1:12.
- ☐ Memorize Lesson 9 Memory Sheet.
- ☐ Say Lesson 9 Memory Sheet out loud from memory in front of a mirror.
- ☐ Say Lesson 9 Memory Sheet to someone before class.
  Have him check the points you remember, listening for accuracy.
- ☐ Hand out five gospel tracts.
- ☐ Pray for the lost and for God's power on your life.
- ☐ Evaluate your Find Five List, continue to actively pursue reaching the people on it, and add new people as needed.

LESSON 9

ONE-PAGE **MEMORY SHEET**

*"Come and see the works of God. . . . I will declare what he hath done for my soul." (Psalm 66:5*a*, 16*b*)*

☐ **CONVERSATION**
I must turn the conversation to the theme of themes.

☐ ① **Making Conversation**
☐ ② **Directing Conversation**
☐ "How would you describe your relationship with God?"
☐ "What do you think it takes to have a relationship with God and live with Him forever in heaven?"
☐ Personal Testimony—He has changed my life.
☐ "Are you 100% sure that all your sins are forgiven and you will go to heaven?"
☐ 1 John 5:13 or Titus 3:5
☐ "May I show you from the Bible how to have a relationship with God?"

☐ **INTRODUCTION**
I must introduce the sinner to the Savior.

☐ ① **God Is Holy** and cannot tolerate our sin.
☐ **God's Intolerance**—Habakkuk 1:13*a*
☐ **God's Reflection**—1 John 3:4*b*
Ten Commandments
☐ **Man's Dilemma**—Romans 3:23
☐ Illustration—Flagpole

☐ ② **God Is Just** and cannot overlook our sin.
☐ **God's Standard**—Romans 6:23*a*
☐ **God's Judgment**—Matthew 25:41
☐ **Man's Destiny**—Revelation 21:8
☐ Illustration—Judge acquitting a proven murderer/brother
"Would that be justice?"

☐ ③ **God Is Loving** and has reached out to us.
☐ He has provided a way for us to be close to Him that satisfies His holy/just nature (John 3:16).
☐ **God's Son**
☐ "Who would you say Jesus is?"
God in flesh—John 1:14
☐ **God's Exchange**—Jesus becomes
☐ Our Substitute—1 Peter 3:18
☐ Our Righteousness—2 Corinthians 5:21
☐ Illustration—My record/His record chart
☐ Our Full Payment—1 John 1:7*b*; John 19:30
☐ **Man's Deliverance** from sin and its penalty —1 Corinthians 15:3–4

☐ ④ **God Is Gracious** and offers salvation as a gift.
☐ **God's Gift**—Ephesians 2:8–9
☐ **God's Offer**—John 1:12
☐ **Man's Decision**
☐ Believe—Acts 16:31
☐ Illustration—Blondine
Get in the wheelbarrow.

The Three Elements of Saving Faith

Understand
God can't tolerate or overlook my sin. He gave His life in exchange for mine and wants to give me eternal life.

Agree
I am a sinner and need a Savior.

Depend/Trust
I choose to receive Jesus' exchange—my sin and its penalty for His record and eternal life.

☐ Illustration—Two chairs
☐ Transfer dependence/trust
☐ Repent—Luke 13:5, change of mind
☐ Illustration—Point of no return
What would you do?

☐ **INVITATION**
I must offer the inquirer the gift of eternal life.

☐ ① **Ask**
☐ "Do you believe that Jesus loves you and will give you forgiveness and eternal life if you ask Him?"
☐ "Then are you willing to receive Him right now?"
☐ ② **Pray**
☐ ③ **Welcome**

☐ **ASSIMILATION**
I must call the disciple to the life of Christ.

LESSON 9

INVITATION

RESOLVE—I MUST OFFER THE INQUIRER THE GIFT OF ETERNAL LIFE.

from the One-Page Memory Sheet

- ☐ ① **Ask**
- ☐ "Do you believe that Jesus loves you and will give you forgiveness and eternal life if you ask Him?"
- ☐ "Are you willing to receive Him right now?"
- ☐ ② **Pray**
- ☐ ③ **Welcome**

POSSIBLE TRANSITION STATEMENT

The last question you asked your friend was what he would do if someone threw him a rope when he was in danger. He probably answered, "I'd grab the rope of safety."

★ Then I have two more questions for you. They are the most important qustions you will every answer.

I. Ask

A. Do you believe that Jesus loves **you** and will give **you** forgiveness and eternal life with Him if you ask Him?

This is an understand-and-agree question.

There have been several times when I thought my friend would say no to this question and was surprised when he said, "Yes, I do."

ED

Ed had a Mormon background. The whole time I was introducing him to God, he kept countering everything I said with Mormon dogma. It wasn't a lack of understanding. He simply did not agree with what I was telling him. I just kept going through the points. To my surprise, when I asked him if he believed that Jesus loved him and would give him forgiveness and eternal life, he said, "Yes!" The Holy Spirit had kept His promise to convince Ed, and he was willing to admit it. Ed didn't get saved that day, but within a couple of weeks he accepted Christ's exchange.

B. Then are you willing to receive Him **right now**?

1. This is where the rubber meets the road. **Don't be afraid to ask this question**. Ask yourself this, "**If Jesus were here, would He ask my friend to receive Him?**"

   *Revelation 3:20—**Behold, I stand at the door, and knock**: if any man hear my voice, and open the door, I will come in to him, and will sup with him, and he with me.*

   *2 Corinthians 5:20—Now then we are ambassadors for Christ, **as though God did beseech [beg] you by us**: we pray [beg] you in Christ's stead [place], be ye reconciled to God.*

   May the cries of hell motivate us to be bold.

   *Luke 16:27–28—Then he said, I pray thee therefore, father [Abraham], that thou wouldest send him [Lazarus] to my father's house: for I have five brethren; that **he may testify unto them**, lest they also come into this place of torment.*

2. It is necessary for the inquirer, your friend, to know that this is the decision point. Until now all he had to decide was to stay engaged in the conversation. He needs to understand that **salvation is not an experience you wait for; it is a decision you make**.

3. If he says yes, lead him in a prayer.

4. If he says no, you will have to depend on God to give you wisdom how to proceed.

   a. It is appropriate to ask him why and to help him sort through the problem.

      If you have gotten this far, you have no doubt seen God working in the situation. He promises that we can be confident "that he which hath begun a good work in you will perform it until the day of Jesus Christ" (Philippians 1:6). **If God is working, He has a plan to bring this to fruition**.

      Nehemiah wrote concerning a quick decision that he had to make while standing before the king, "So I prayed to the God of heaven. **And I said** . . ." (Nehemiah 2:4*b*-5*a*).

      This is the time for you to **pray and say** what God leads you to say. Trust Him. Look to Him. **He will give you wisdom**!

      MARY ELLEN

      Mary Ellen had been saved for a little over two years and had seen several people saved while studying *The Exchange* Bible study, but she had always participated in the studies with my wife and me. She had been praying for her family since her own salvation, and now her daughter had finally agreed to do *The Exchange* Bible study with her. After lesson 1 she got nervous and called to see if we could go with her the next time. She said it was time to "call in the big guns." I reminded her that she had the big guns. The Holy Spirit was in her and would lead her.

      She continued the Bible study by herself, though she was still nervous. When she saw her daughter struggling with the decision to trust Christ as her Lord and Savior, she told her, "Darlin', I know you well enough to know that you are thinking God has you at the edge of a cliff and is asking you to jump off into a black abyss. That's not what He's asking you to do at all. Christ is standing right in front of you. All He is asking you to do is simply step into His outstretched arms."

      God gave her the wisdom she needed to lead her own adult daughter to Him.

      1) Sometimes there is a simple lack of understanding that can be cleared up and the decision can then be made.

2) Sometimes your friend is expecting an experience, and he doesn't think he "feels" ready. Remind him that salvation is not an experience you wait for; it is a decision you make.

3) Sometimes your friend is afraid that getting saved will mean some loved one who has already gone to eternity will never be seen again or that he is admitting that the loved one didn't go to heaven.

- Assure your friend that we don't know where the loved one is. He might have been saved.
- Assure your friend that no matter what, he can be sure his loved one would want him to make this decision (remember the rich man's cry from hell?).

4) Sometimes he is simply procrastinating.

*2 Corinthians 6:2*b—*Behold, now is the accepted time; behold, now is the day of salvation.*

Proverbs 27:1—Boast not thyself of to morrow; for thou knowest not what a day may bring forth.

5) Sometimes he is reluctant to turn from his sin.

John 3:19—And this is the condemnation, that light is come into the world, and men loved darkness rather than light, because their deeds were evil.

Often a person is not willing to admit that this is the problem. Many intellectual arguments are more about holding onto sin than about the specific argument. It may be appropriate to ask if this might be the problem.

b. In some cases it may be appropriate at this point to simply ask him to do the *The Exchange* Bible study. (**The vast majority** of genuine inquirers who complete all four lessons either get saved or gain assurance of salvation.)

1) Don't let rejection cause you to back off and lose your boldness.

2) At the same time, don't let yourself become impatient either.

a) Nicodemus and Joseph of Arimathaea both became believers well after Jesus first dealt with them.

b) The parable of the sower and the seed indicates that sometimes it takes patience to see fruit harvested.

Mark 4:26–29—And he said, So is the kingdom of God, as if a man should cast seed into the ground; and should sleep, and rise night and day, and the seed should spring and grow up, he knoweth not how. For the earth bringeth forth fruit of herself; first the blade, then the ear, after that the full corn in the ear. But when the fruit is brought forth, immediately he putteth in the sickle, because the harvest is come.

It also indicates that the reason the stony ground sprang up so quickly was that it was shallow soil (Mark 4:2–8, 14–20).

Is it possible that the reason we don't see many of the people we lead to the Lord come to church and go on to serve the Lord is that our methods are aimed primarily at shallow soil? The indication is that good soil will respond to the seed more slowly.

Be careful! We don't want to get to the point that we don't expect to see fruit. That was clearly not the attitude of this farmer. He was watching night and day. When the fruit was ripe, he was immediately ready to harvest it.

II. Pray

A. This invitation is similar to the ones you have heard in church.

1. Finish the gospel presentation.

2. Ask the closing questions that bring your friend to a decision.

3. Invite your friend to express his faith in Jesus.

4. Welcome the new convert into the family of God.

5. Begin discipleship.

B. Be prepared. This is the time the enemy attacks most severely.

C. Some people have never heard a real prayer.

1. Some have never heard another person pray before.

2. Some have heard only prayers read from a prayer book.

D. Ask the Lord for wisdom to lead your friend to pray.

1. It is a privilege to hear your friend pray in his own words.

★ You can tell him to "Just talk to God and tell Him what is on your heart. Tell God you want to receive the exchange He has offered you."

It may be helpful to review what he is going to pray using the three elements of saving faith.

The Three Elements of Saving Faith

Understand
God can't tolerate or overlook my sin. He gave His life in exchange for mine and wants to give me eternal life.

Agree
I am a sinner and need a Savior.

Depend/Trust
I choose to receive Jesus' exchange—my sin and its penalty for His record and eternal life.

ED

Ed had been in church for many years and had always thought he was good enough to get to heaven. He would often tell me about the good things he was doing to get to heaven. Finally one day the Holy Spirit had finished His work in Ed's heart, and Ed responded to a public invitation when a guest speaker was preaching. I dealt with Ed myself. He assured me that he was ready to trust Christ alone for the forgiveness of his sins. He agreed to pray to place his faith in Him, but when he started praying, he got stuck in his old pattern. He started, "Dear God, you know I've tried to be good. I've always gone to church and given my money and . . ."

I interrupted him and asked, "Ed, were you going to tell Him you are a sinner and that you need forgiveness of sins made possible only through Christ's death and resurrection?"

He snapped out of the routine prayer and prayed a lovely sinner's prayer. **Sometimes your friend will need a little help praying**.

ROSS

Ross came to the Lord in adverse circumstances. When I went to visit him in the hospital, he was none too happy to see me there with his parents. We started to share the gospel that night, and the Lord obviously worked in his life, but I didn't get a chance to finish. We agreed to meet again the next day. When I finished the gospel presentation, Ross said yes, he was ready to ask Christ to save him. When I began to review what he was going to tell the Lord, he interrupted and sternly said, "This is my prayer!" He bowed his head and began praying. I have never seen anyone so broken over sin or so violently enter into the kingdom of heaven. Tears were splashing on the kitchen table as he prayed. **Sometimes your friend won't need any help**.

2. There are times when it is better to have him repeat a simple prayer after you.

    a. Some people are shy and the pressure to pray is a little too great. Repeating a prayer after you helps remove your friend's nervousness so they can focus on placing their trust in Christ.

    b. Remind your friend that it is not the words but the dependence that is important. You can say the following:

    ★ "You and God know if you are sincere, and that's what counts."

    c. When you lead him in prayer, it is helpful to tailor his prayer to deal with his specific needs.

    d. If you have him repeat after you, make the prayer simple, add pauses for him to pray, and go slowly enough for him to think about what he is saying.

    e. The *Giving the Exchange* Gospel Presentation System (GPS) has this sample prayer on the last panel. (Go to www.exchangemessage.org.)

Dear Jesus,

I have sinned against Your holy nature and deserve judgment in hell. I believe that You loved me enough to die in my place. Please forgive my sins, exchange my sinful record for Your holy one, and give me eternal life in heaven. Thank You, Jesus. Amen.

E. Close in prayer as soon as your friend is done.

III. Welcome

A. ★ Let me be the first one to welcome you to the family of God.

1. Be warm and genuine.

2. Your friend is bound to be excited. Match his enthusiasm with your own.

B. It is sometimes appropriate to ask some questions that might solidify the decision.

★ What did you just do?

★ What did God do?

★ If you were to die right now, where would you go?

- ★ If you had died yesterday before you made this decision, where would you have gone?
- ★ Your decision made a big difference, didn't it?
- ★ If you die five years from now, where will you go?

Don't panic if your convert doesn't answer everything correctly. Simply keep on teaching the reality of what just happened and the unchanging nature of the promises of God.

LESSON 10

ASSIGNMENT SHEET

- ☐ Complete the On the Job Training Debriefing Chart for last week's encounters.
- ☐ Pray with your prayer partners.
- ☐ Read Lesson 10, "Assimilation."
- ☐ Read chapters 28–30 from *Just What the Doctor Ordered.*
- ☐ Memorize Acts 16:31 and Luke 13:5.
- ☐ Memorize Lesson 10 Memory Sheet.
- ☐ Say Lesson 10 Memory Sheet out loud from memory in front of a mirror.
- ☐ Say Lesson 10 Memory Sheet to someone before class.
  Have him check the points you remember, listening for accuracy.
- ☐ Hand out five gospel tracts.
- ☐ Pray for the lost and for God's power on your life.
- ☐ Evaluate your Find Five List, continue to actively pursue reaching the people on it, and add new people as needed.

LESSON 10

ONE-PAGE **MEMORY SHEET**

*"Come and see the works of God. . . . I will declare what he hath done for my soul." (Psalm 66:5*a*, 16*b*)*

☐ **CONVERSATION**
I must turn the conversation to the theme of themes.

☐ ① **Making Conversation**
☐ ② **Directing Conversation**
☐ "How would you describe your relationship with God?"
☐ "What do you think it takes to have a relationship with God and live with Him forever in heaven?"
☐ Personal Testimony—He has changed my life.
☐ "Are you 100% sure that all your sins are forgiven and you will go to heaven?"
☐ 1 John 5:13 or Titus 3:5
☐ "May I show you from the Bible how to have a relationship with God?"

☐ **INTRODUCTION**
I must introduce the sinner to the Savior.

☐ ① **God Is Holy** and cannot tolerate our sin.
☐ **God's Intolerance**—Habakkuk 1:13*a*
☐ **God's Reflection**—1 John 3:4*b*
Ten Commandments
☐ **Man's Dilemma**—Romans 3:23
☐ Illustration—Flagpole

☐ ② **God Is Just** and cannot overlook our sin.
☐ **God's Standard**—Romans 6:23*a*
☐ **God's Judgment**—Matthew 25:41
☐ **Man's Destiny**—Revelation 21:8
☐ Illustration—Judge acquitting a proven murderer/brother
"Would that be justice?"

☐ ③ **God Is Loving** and has reached out to us.
☐ He has provided a way for us to be close to Him that satisfies His holy/just nature (John 3:16).
☐ **God's Son**
☐ "Who would you say Jesus is?"
God in flesh—John 1:14
☐ **God's Exchange**—Jesus becomes
☐ Our Substitute—1 Peter 3:18
☐ Our Righteousness—2 Corinthians 5:21
☐ Illustration—My record/His record chart
☐ Our Full Payment—1 John 1:7*b*; John 19:30
☐ **Man's Deliverance** from sin and its penalty —1 Corinthians 15:3–4

☐ ④ **God Is Gracious** and offers salvation as a gift.
☐ **God's Gift**—Ephesians 2:8–9
☐ **God's Offer**—John 1:12
☐ **Man's Decision**
☐ Believe—Acts 16:31
☐ Illustration—Blondine
Get in the wheelbarrow.

The Three Elements of Saving Faith

Understand
God can't tolerate or overlook my sin. He gave His life in exchange for mine and wants to give me eternal life.

Agree
I am a sinner and need a Savior.

Depend/Trust
I choose to receive Jesus' exchange—my sin and its penalty for His record and eternal life.

☐ Illustration—Two chairs
☐ Transfer dependence/trust
☐ Repent—Luke 13:5, change of mind
☐ Illustration—Point of no return
What would you do?

☐ **INVITATION**
I must offer the inquirer the gift of eternal life.

☐ ① **Ask**
☐ "Do you believe that Jesus loves you and will give you forgiveness and eternal life if you ask Him?"
☐ "Then are you willing to receive Him right now?"
☐ ② **Pray**
☐ ③ **Welcome**

☐ **ASSIMILATION**
I must call the disciple to the life of Christ.

☐ ① **Assurance**—John 5:24
☐ ② **Acceptance**—Ephesians 1:6*b*
☐ ③ **Adoption**—Romans 8:15*b*
☐ Heavenly family/Holy Spirit
☐ Church family/Church attendance
☐ ④ **Inheritance**
☐ His Victory—1 Corinthians 15:57
☐ His Life— Galatians 2:20
☐ His Word—1 Peter 2:2
☐ ***Living the Exchange:*** *A Disciple's Bible Study*

LESSON 10

ASSIMILATION

RESOLVE: I MUST CALL THE DISCIPLE TO THE LIFE OF CHRIST.

from the One-Page Memory Sheet

- ☐ ① **Assurance**—John 5:24
- ☐ ② **Acceptance**—Ephesians 1:6*b*
- ☐ ③ **Adoption**—Romans 8:15*b*
- ☐ Heavenly family/Holy Spirit
- ☐ Church family/church attendance
- ☐ ④ **Inheritance**
- ☐ His victory—1 Corinthians 15:57
- ☐ His life—Galatians 2:20
- ☐ His Word—1 Peter 2:2
- ☐ ***Living the Exchange***: *A Disciple's Bible Study*

Two pictures from science help us understand the concept of assimilation.

• Assimilation has occurred when the body converts nutrients into the very fabric of its living tissue.

• Assimilation has occurred when sugar is dissolved into iced tea. Until then, the sugar and tea are still two separate parts in a mixture. If you stop stirring, the sugar ends up in the bottom of the glass.

Your disciple is still a visitor and highly vulnerable until he is actually assimilated into the very fabric of a church family. God's plan is for every Christian to be an assimilated member of a good, Bible-preaching church. Your job in evangelism and discipleship isn't done until you see your friend assimilated into your church, if at all possible.

2 Timothy 2:2—And the things that thou hast heard of me among many witnesses, the same commit thou to faithful men, who shall be able to teach others also.

Dawson Trotman wrote a little booklet entitled *Born to Reproduce*. The complete circle of ministry that Paul taught to Timothy is the same one we should pursue with our converts. The first step is to begin personal discipleship, but we must quickly see him assimilated into the church and growing independently.

Relationship is the key to effective assimilation.

MICHAEL

Michael and Renee both made decisions while studying *The Exchange* Bible study. My wife and I and Michael's close friend Mary Ellen had done the Bible study with them weekly for over a month. After their decisions, they were both baptized, and then their oldest son was saved and baptized. They are now in church "every time the doors were opened." Michael and I were talking about how quickly he had become assimilated into the church. I suggested it was because he already had a relationship with Mary Ellen. His reply was a pleasant surprise, "I knew you too. You had been over to our house at least five times by then. I knew that if I didn't know anyone at church, I could always hang out with you."

More than the kind of music, the style of the service, and the types of programs, relationships with friends in the church family keep new believers in church.

POSSIBLE TRANSITION STATEMENT

★ Now that you are a part of the family of God, I have a booklet I'd like to give you that shows you a little bit of the huge difference Jesus has made in your life.

Note: This section has been put into a booklet entitled *An Invitation to* Living the Exchange. You can find it at www.exchangemessage.org. If you use the booklet, you won't have to teach every part of the assimilation section. You should highlight the main points as you point them out in the booklet to motivate the new disciple to read it right away.

I always try to get a commitment that the new convert will attend church the next Sunday, and I at least introduce *Living the Exchange: A Disciple's Bible Study*. I usually tell him that I will get back with him to see if he will do the Bible study.

The Evil One is loathe to give up one he has held captive, and he will do all he can to attack your friend. I have never met a victorious Christian who doubted his salvation. This is one of the first areas Satan will attack as he strives to stymie the growth of your friend. Mark 4 teaches that Satan snatches the seed away from those who do not receive the Word and aims affliction and persecution at the heart of new converts where the Word has taken root, attempting to make them unproductive. We can arm them for these attacks by teaching them these principles.

This outline is written as you should teach it to your convert.

I. Assurance

John 5:24—Verily, verily [truly, truly], I [Jesus] say unto you, he that heareth my word, and believeth on him that sent me, hath everlasting life, and shall not come into condemnation; but is passed from death unto life.

★ This is a long verse, but it really has only two parts—your responsibility and God's promise.

A. Your responsibility—Jesus asks two things of you. It is important that your disciple is able to comfortably answer yes to both of these questions.

   1. Did you listen to God's Word concerning Jesus' gift of forgiveness and eternal life?

   2. Did you choose to depend on the truth that God sent Jesus to die in your place?

B. God's promise

1. You **have** eternal life.

   Notice it doesn't say **you will have** eternal life in the future. It says you possess it right now!

   ★ How long does eternal life last? (Forever!)

   ★ When did you get eternal life? (The moment you chose to trust in Jesus!)

   ★ When will your eternal life end? (Never! Right now you are eternally safe in Jesus.)

2. You will never come into condemnation.

   Remember the passages of the Bible that show the just judgment of God on those who are condemned to hell? You will never have to face that condemnation. You'll never have to worry about that again.

   You can be sure of this because of the next promise.

3. You have passed from spiritual death, with no ability to please God, to spiritual life. A tremendous change has taken place in your life.

   You now have what is necessary to please Him. You may not always feel as though this is true, but your feelings don't change the fact that it is true! You can count on God's Word! Remember, God cannot lie. His Word is always true.

   Jesus said, "Heaven and earth shall pass away, but my words shall not pass away" (Matthew 24:35).

   There should be a genuine growing excitement between the two of you at this point.

II. Acceptance

*Ephesians 1:6*b—*He hath made us accepted in the beloved.*

A. You are fully accepted by God.

B. When Jesus was here on earth, God actually spoke from heaven on two different occasions and said, "This is my beloved Son, in whom I am well pleased" (Matthew 3:17*b*; 17:5*b*).

   1. Remember, God is Holy! The only human God has ever been completely pleased with is Jesus, because He alone is truly holy.

   2. The word *accepted* in Ephesians 1:6 carries with it the meaning that we are now well pleasing through the gift of Christ's redemption by His grace.

C. It is hard to imagine, but the Bible teaches that you are as accepted in heaven as Christ is because you have been placed into Christ.

   When you made your exchange with Jesus, He gave you His righteousness. You are accepted in Him, because you are in Him.

   *Colossians 3:3*b–*4*a—*Your life is hid with Christ in God. . . . Christ . . . is our life.*

   This truth is a great tool to help a person gain freedom from lingering feelings of guilt.

III. Adoption

*Romans 8:15*b—*Ye have received the Spirit of adoption, whereby we cry, Abba, Father.*

A. You have a new heavenly family.

1. The Bible teaches that you have been adopted into God's family.

   a. The word *abba* is an endearing word for *father*, similar to our use of the word *daddy*.

      ISRAEL
      A few years ago my wife and I went to Israel, where we visited the headwaters of the Jordan River on a national holiday. The water from this beautiful place comes bubbling up out of the ground and forms a natural pool before it spills down through the Jordan Valley. Because it was a holiday, several Israeli families were visiting this inviting place. Through the blur of a foreign language one word rang out clearly to our ears. It was the word *Abba*, as the little children frolicked in the water and called to their fathers to watch them or to play with them.

   b. God has allowed you to have an intimate relationship with Him.

   c. As a close family member you can appeal directly to His throne.

      Imagine the child of the king being able to run right past the guards that keep others out to ask his daddy for help with some trivial problem. This is the relationship we have been given with the King of Kings, and the Lord of Lords.

2. In addition to this, God has also placed His Holy Spirit inside of you to help you call out to God in time of need.

There is an obvious parallel between the spiritual family of God and the importance of the practical benefits of the church family.

B. You have a new church family.

★ God has also given you a family here on earth to help you grow spiritually. It is your church family.

1. God marvelously built the church to help us stay excited and zealous for Him.

   ILLUSTRATION
   Picture a log fire burning brightly in a cozy fireplace. Now imagine taking one of the logs out and setting it on the hearth. What do you think will happen? That log will probably stop burning, start smoking, and make a mess. If you take the same log and put it back in the fireplace where it belongs, it will once again burn brightly and help warm the room. In a similar way, God has built the church to help you stay on fire and useful for the Lord. When people get out of church, they tend to lose their zeal and make a mess of God's plan for their lives. When Christians stay in church, as God intended, they tend to grow in their spiritual walk and usefulness to God.

2. *Hebrews 10:25—Not forsaking the assembling of ourselves together [attending church], as the manner of some is; but exhorting [building up] one another: and so much the more, as ye see the day approaching.*

   Christians who decide to be active in church usually grow rapidly in their relationship with God, and those who don't stay active rarely keep growing.

   The more a person is involved in church the faster he tends to grow!

Invite the new disciple to church for the following Sunday morning. Offer to pick him up. Encourage him to make a decision right now to begin a pattern of faithful attendance in church.

IV. Inheritance

Most Christians are not aware of the vast inheritance that became theirs when they received Christ. Express your excitement when you show the new convert the first few gifts that are now his in Christ. Remind him that these gifts are his by right of the exchange he made with Jesus.

A. **His victory**. You have been gifted with the victory of Jesus.

1 Corinthians 15:57—But thanks be to God, which ***giveth us*** *the victory through our Lord Jesus Christ.*

It has been said that the only human to ever live the victorious Christian life is Jesus, but notice what this verse teaches about us! The victorious life of Christ **has been** given to you.

1. God promises that there is not a single temptation that can come into your life that He will not give you the ability to resist.

   1 Corinthians 10:13—There hath no temptation taken you but such as is common to man: but God is faithful, who will not suffer you to be tempted above that ye are able; but will with the temptation also make a way to escape, that ye may be able to bear it.

2. Though we participate in victory by our choices, it is a gift. Just like salvation, we cannot earn it.

   ILLUSTRATION

   This victory is like salvation in that it is part of the inheritance rights you gained when you accepted Christ as your Savior. Like money that has been placed into an account for you, victory already belongs to you, and you can claim it as you need it by steps of faith.

B. **His life**. You have been given His life.

Galatians 2:20—I am crucified with Christ: nevertheless I live; yet not I, but ***Christ liveth in me****: and the life which I now live in the flesh I live by the faith of the Son of God, who loved me, and gave himself for me.*

1. **Your** old record and **inability to please God died with Jesus** on the cross.

2. In a similar way, as Jesus was bodily resurrected here on earth, you received new life from Him.

   a. He **is** eternal life.

      1 John 1:2—For the life was manifested, and we have seen it [Him], and bear witness, and shew unto you that eternal life, which was with the Father, and was manifested unto us.

   b. When you received Him, you received eternal life. Now He wants to **live His life in you**.

   c. This right was given to you at salvation and is practiced now by faith that enables obedience.

C. **His Word**. One of the greatest gifts you have been given is the Word of God.

1 Peter 2:2—As newborn babes, desire the sincere milk of the word, that ye may grow thereby.

1. The Bible is your lifeline to Jesus and His life-sustaining strength.

   New babies have a voracious appetite and an amazing capacity to grow, but they are also very susceptible to extreme health problems if for some reason they do not eat sufficiently. As a new Christian these same facts are true about you in a spiritual sense.

   If you choose to nourish yourself through reading, memorizing, studying, and hearing God's Word, you will receive His strength to grow in your relationship with God. **But beware**. If you neglect God's Word, you will be extremely vulnerable to spiritual danger.

2. The Bible is a library of books, and a great book to read first is the Gospel of John. It deals primarily with Jesus' life here on earth. The Holy Spirit led John to close this book by saying that there were many other things Jesus did while here on earth that were not recorded, "but these are written, **that ye might believe** that Jesus is the Christ, the Son of God; and that believing **ye might have life** through his name" (John 20:31).

V. *Living the Exchange: A Disciple's Bible Study*

A. *Living the Exchange* is a twelve-lesson Bible study that will help you begin to live this new life in Christ.

B. Every Christian must learn to live out of the inheritance he has received through the exchange he made with Christ. He needs to grow in his relationship with God as his Father, Master, Lord, friend, and partner.

End the visit by confirming the new Christian's plan to be in church on Sunday and ask if you can close in prayer. All this material in the "Assimilation" lesson is covered in *Living the Exchange*. If you are not able to cover it all, make sure to invite him to church and tell him about the Bible study, *Living the Exchange*.

SECTION 3

SUMMARY

LESSON 11

ASSIGNMENT SHEET

- ☐ Complete the On the Job Training Debriefing Chart, for last week's encounters.
- ☐ Pray with your prayer partners.
- ☐ Read Lesson 11, "Practical Advice for Effective Soulwinners."
- ☐ Read chapters 31–33 from *Just What the Doctor Ordered.*
- ☐ Review the mandatory memory verses.
- ☐ Review Lesson 11 Memory Sheet.
- ☐ Give the entire gospel presentation out loud from memory in front of a mirror. (You may refer to the GPS or One-Page Memory Sheet as needed.)
- ☐ Give the entire gospel presentation to someone before class. (You may use the GPS or One-Page Memory Sheet.)
  Have him check the points you remember on the Lesson 11 Memory Sheet, listening for accuracy.
- ☐ Hand out five gospel tracts.
- ☐ Pray for the lost and for God's power on your life.
- ☐ Evaluate your Find Five List, continue to actively pursue reaching the people on it, and add new people as needed.

LESSON 11

ONE-PAGE **MEMORY SHEET**

"Come and see the works of God. . . . I will declare what he hath done for my soul." (Psalm 66:5a, 16b)

☐ **CONVERSATION**
I must turn the conversation to the theme of themes.

☐ ① **Making Conversation**
☐ ② **Directing Conversation**
☐ "How would you describe your relationship with God?"
☐ "What do you think it takes to have a relationship with God and live with Him forever in heaven?"
☐ Personal Testimony—He has changed my life.
☐ "Are you 100% sure that all your sins are forgiven and you will go to heaven?"
☐ 1 John 5:13 or Titus 3:5
☐ "May I show you from the Bible how to have a relationship with God?"

☐ **INTRODUCTION**
I must introduce the sinner to the Savior.

☐ ① **God Is Holy** and cannot tolerate our sin.
☐ **God's Intolerance**—Habakkuk 1:13*a*
☐ **God's Reflection**—1 John 3:4*b*
Ten Commandments
☐ **Man's Dilemma**—Romans 3:23
☐ Illustration—Flagpole

☐ ② **God Is Just** and cannot overlook our sin.
☐ **God's Standard**—Romans 6:23*a*
☐ **God's Judgment**—Matthew 25:41
☐ **Man's Destiny**—Revelation 21:8
☐ Illustration—Judge acquitting a proven murderer/brother
"Would that be justice?"

☐ ③ **God Is Loving** and has reached out to us.
☐ He has provided a way for us to be close to Him that satisfies His holy/just nature (John 3:16).
☐ **God's Son**
☐ "Who would you say Jesus is?"
God in flesh—John 1:14
☐ **God's Exchange**—Jesus becomes
☐ Our Substitute—1 Peter 3:18
☐ Our Righteousness—2 Corinthians 5:21
☐ Illustration—My record/His record chart
☐ Our Full Payment—1 John 1:7*b*; John 19:30
☐ **Man's Deliverance** from sin and its penalty —1 Corinthians 15:3–4

☐ ④ **God Is Gracious** and offers salvation as a gift.
☐ **God's Gift**—Ephesians 2:8–9
☐ **God's Offer**—John 1:12
☐ **Man's Decision**
☐ Believe—Acts 16:31
☐ Illustration—Blondine
Get in the wheelbarrow.

The Three Elements of Saving Faith

Understand
God can't tolerate or overlook my sin. He gave His life in exchange for mine and wants to give me eternal life.

Agree
I am a sinner and need a Savior.

Depend/Trust
I choose to receive Jesus' exchange—my sin and its penalty for His record and eternal life.

☐ Illustration—Two chairs
☐ Transfer dependence/trust
☐ Repent—Luke 13:5, change of mind
☐ Illustration—Point of no return
What would you do?

☐ **INVITATION**
I must offer the inquirer the gift of eternal life.

☐ ① **Ask**
☐ "Do you believe that Jesus loves you and will give you forgiveness and eternal life if you ask Him?"
☐ "Then are you willing to receive Him right now?"
☐ ② **Pray**
☐ ③ **Welcome**

☐ **ASSIMILATION**
I must call the disciple to the life of Christ.

☐ ① **Assurance**—John 5:24
☐ ② **Acceptance**—Ephesians 1:6*b*
☐ ③ **Adoption**—Romans 8:15*b*
☐ Heavenly family/Holy Spirit
☐ Church family/Church attendance
☐ ④ **Inheritance**
☐ His Victory—1 Corinthians 15:57
☐ His Life— Galatians 2:20
☐ His Word—1 Peter 2:2
☐ ***Living the Exchange:*** *A Disciple's Bible Study*

LESSON 11

PRACTICAL ADVICE FOR EFFECTIVE SOULWINNERS

I. Depend on the Holy Spirit for boldness.

Acts 4:29, 31—And now, Lord, behold their threatenings: and grant unto thy servants, that with all boldness they may speak thy word, . . . and when they had prayed . . . they spake the word of God with boldness.

A. Determine to turn conversations to the theme of themes.

> **I resolve to direct every conversation I possibly can to the theme of themes, learn of that soul's need, and if possible meet it.**

B. When you are doing On the Job Training be sure to ask, "May we come in?"

II. Try to create a comfortable setting when making a visit.

A. Ask, "Where would you like us to sit?"

B. Do your best to have the person who is going to present the gospel sit as close to your new friend as possible.

C. Prepare each team member for his role before you get to the visit.

D. Utilize the role of a silent partner.

E. Utilize Tossing the Presentation tools.

1. The first few attempts at participating in the presentation can be difficult. The trainer should plan to get into the presentation and then calmly say, "________ (trainee's name) has been studying God's holiness. ________ (trainee's name) why don't you tell ________ (friend's name) what you have learned?"

2. When the trainee has gone as far as he can, teach him to simply ask, "________ (trainer's name) do you have anything you would like to add to that?"

   While this may be code for "Help" your new friend hears only that you have finished talking about what you have studied.

III. Make friends.

A. Remember that one of the first goals of each visit is to demonstrate your love and concern and to make redemptive relationships.

B. Look for friends everywhere you go. Show the love of Jesus to everyone you meet. Our job is to manifest Him to those around us. Practice smiling at people as you pass them. They may never know, but Jesus is behind that smile.

C. Actively pursue redemptive relationships. Keep your Find Five list current.

IV. Ask the Lord to teach you to let your only offense be the gospel, not your personality, mannerisms, or idiosyncrasies.

A. Attempt to make your life and appearance attractive to those the Lord is calling to Himself.

*1 Corinthians 9:19*b, *22*b—*I made myself* ***servant unto all****, that I might gain the more. . . . I am made* ***all things to all men, that I might by all means save some****.*

B. When you are making visits for your church, you are representing both your church and the Lord. Be sure to dress appropriately. (Wear nice clothes, but avoid overdressing. Wearing a tie or "Sunday clothes" in a casual setting makes people uncomfortable.)

C. Don't allow yourself to be distracted by your surroundings.

D. Be a good listener. Don't talk too much, especially about yourself. Show genuine interest and concern.

E. Be natural. Don't be stiff or contrived as though you are going through a memorized spiel.

F. Learn from your On the Job Training debriefing times.

V. Mold your expectations to the Word of God.

A. Expect divine appointments.

B. Expect God to use you.

C. Don't expect to **feel** strong. We are weak. Only He is strong!

*2 Corinthians 12:9*a—*And he said unto me, My grace is sufficient for thee: for* ***my strength is made perfect in weakness****.*

D. Expect occasional rejection.

*John 15:18–20*a—*If the world hate you, ye know that it hated me before it hated you. If ye were of the world, the world would love his own: but because ye are not of the world, but I have chosen you out of the world, therefore the world hateth you. Remember the word that I said unto you,* ***The servant is not greater than his lord. If they have persecuted me, they will also persecute you****.*

E. Pray for and expect God's power.

VI. Live in the realities of 2 Corinthians 2:14–17.

Now thanks be unto God, which ***always causeth us to triumph*** *in Christ, and* ***maketh manifest the savour [fragrance] of his knowledge by us in every place****. For we are unto God a sweet savour of Christ, in them that are saved, and in them that perish: to the one we are the savour of death unto death; and to the other the savour of life unto life. And who is sufficient for these things? For we are not as many, which corrupt the word of God: but as of sincerity, but as of God, in the sight of God speak we in Christ.*

A. Expect the invisible, powerful, invasive, subtle presence of Christ in you to make an impact on your friend.

1. When you are filled with the Spirit of Christ, He will draw men to Himself through you. Christ promises to manifest His invisible, powerful aura through you.

2. This passage also indicates that those who refuse the gospel will find the fragrance of Christ in you as repulsive as the pungent stench of death. It is no wonder the world hates powerful Christianity, and it is no wonder Paul had to ask for boldness, knowing how some would reject him.

B. Beware of peddling the Word of God. Hucksters use corrupt methods. They put their best "fruit" on top of the basket while hiding less desirable fruit underneath. If we try to get a person to church with something other than Christ, **where does that relegate Him**?

C. Be sincere. Have **genuine, valuable integrity**.

D. Speak in Christ!

"**Speak we**"—The tongue is ours, but the power is God's.

In Christ—"Words which He gives, approves, and blesses." —John Wesley

VII. Don't discredit the gospel or get distracted.

A. Sin will hinder your effectiveness.

*Hebrews 12:1*b*—Let us **lay aside every weight, and** the **sin** which doth so easily beset us, and let us run with patience the race that is set before us.*

B. Many things must be laid aside if we are going to have time—not to mention **a heart—for Great Commission living**.

Mark 4:19—And the cares of this world, and the deceitfulness of riches, and the lusts of other things entering in, choke the word, and it becometh unfruitful.

VIII. Watch for the Lord's leading.

Proverbs 28:26—He that trusteth in his own heart is a fool.

IX. Keep moving; find souls; use all the time you have.

X. Trust the Holy Spirit and the power of the gospel.

A. The Holy Spirit has promised to convince people if we will be His channels. You don't have to rely primarily on apologetics when your reliance is on Him.

John 16:8—And when he [the Holy Spirit] is come, he will reprove the world of sin, and of righteousness, and of judgment.

B. God has promised to do His work in the hearts of men as we articulate the gospel through the Word of God.

*Romans 1:16*a*—For I am not ashamed of **the gospel** of Christ: for it **is the power of God unto salvation** to every one that believeth.*

*Romans 10:17—So then **faith cometh by hearing**, and hearing by **the word of God**.*

*1 Corinthians 1:21—For after that in the wisdom of God the world by wisdom knew not God, **it pleased God by the foolishness of preaching to save** them that believe.*

*Hebrews 4:12—For **the word of God is quick [alive], and powerful [effective]**, and sharper than any twoedged sword, piercing even to the dividing asunder of soul and spirit, and of the joints and marrow, and is a discerner of the thoughts and intents of the heart.*

ILLUSTRATION

Imagine a thief trying to rob a bank and laughing at a security guard who accosts him with a gun, saying, "I don't believe that is a real gun!" How would the guard prove that the gun is powerful and effective? He would simply have to pull the trigger, and the thief would receive the full impact of the weapon.

If someone scoffs at you and says he doesn't believe the Bible, all you have to do is—"pull the trigger"—show him the truth from the Bible and the Holy Spirit will do the convincing.

CHRIS

Chris came to my office on her way to commit suicide. I told her the good news that Jesus loved her and died for her, but she could not believe that Jesus could love her because she felt so wicked. She had been abused most of her life and could not imagine anyone actually loving her. I told her the story of the woman at the well, pointing out that even though she had had five husbands and was living with a man out of wedlock, Jesus went through Samaria for the express purpose of looking for her. She replied, "Why isn't He looking for me?"

I assured her that He was. I showed her Romans 3:10–11, "As it is written, There is none righteous, no, not one: there is none that understandeth, there is none that seeketh after God." I told her that in the flesh no one desires to read the Bible and come to church. Her desire for those things proved that Jesus loved her and was looking for her as surely as He had the woman at the well. The words registered in her mind but would not penetrate her wounded heart. She asked, "How can I know that?"

God gave me these words: "The Author of this book is still alive, and He is telling you it's true right now in your heart, isn't He?"

With tears streaming down her face, she smiled slightly, raised her eyes to meet mine, and nodded in agreement. Several days later she was gloriously saved and later baptized. Her estranged husband came to see her baptism and got right with the Lord. They were eventually reunited.

ROB

When I met Rob, he had been committed to a mental ward for planning to commit suicide. He was anything but trusting; in fact, he was angry that I was there.

He agreed to listen to the gospel but was clearly scoffing at the truth. As we were talking about sin and hell, he asked with a sneer, "How do you know that's true?"

I told him all I had to do was give him the gospel, and the Spirit of God would work in his heart to convince him. I went on to tell him how the Holy Spirit works. "He doesn't speak to you out loud. It's kind of like hearing a small voice inside telling you, 'That's true, that's true.' Or sometimes you feel like something is squeezing your heart."

He replied, "Maybe that's why I've felt weird from the moment you came in here."

Rob was soon released from the mental ward, and I met with him again. He answered the Holy Spirit's voice and entered the kingdom of heaven.

XI. Develop a lifestyle of making soulwinning contacts.

2 Corinthians 5:20—Now then we are ambassadors for Christ, as though God did beseech you by us: ***we pray [beg] you in Christ's stead****, be ye reconciled to God.*

LESSON 12

ASSIGNMENT SHEET

- ☐ Complete the On the Job Training Debriefing Chart for last week's encounters.
- ☐ Pray with your prayer partners.
- ☐ Read Lesson 12, "General Knowledge Review."
- ☐ Read chapters 31–33 from *Just What the Doctor Ordered.*
- ☐ Prepare for the mandatory memory verses test. (This may be downloaded at www.exchangemessage.org.)
- ☐ Review Lesson 11 Memory Sheet.
- ☐ Give the entire gospel presentation out loud from memory in front of a mirror. (refer to the GPS or One-Page Memory Sheet as needed)
- ☐ Give the entire gospel presentation to someone before class. (You can use the GPS or One-Page Memory Sheet.) Have him check the points you remember on the Lesson 11 Memory Sheet, listening for accuracy.
- ☐ Hand out five gospel tracts.
- ☐ Pray for the lost and for God's power on your life.
- ☐ Evaluate your Find Five List, continue to actively pursue reaching the people on it, and add new people as needed.

LESSON 12

ONE-PAGE **MEMORY SHEET**

*"Come and see the works of God. . . . I will declare what he hath done for my soul." (Psalm 66:5*a*, 16*b*)*

☐ **CONVERSATION**
I must turn the conversation to the theme of themes.

☐ ① **Making Conversation**
☐ ② **Directing Conversation**
☐ "How would you describe your relationship with God?"
☐ "What do you think it takes to have a relationship with God and live with Him forever in heaven?"
☐ Personal Testimony—He has changed my life.
☐ "Are you 100% sure that all your sins are forgiven and you will go to heaven?"
☐ 1 John 5:13 or Titus 3:5
☐ "May I show you from the Bible how to have a relationship with God?"

☐ **INTRODUCTION**
I must introduce the sinner to the Savior.

☐ ① **God Is Holy** and cannot tolerate our sin.
☐ **God's Intolerance**—Habakkuk 1:13*a*
☐ **God's Reflection**—1 John 3:4*b*
Ten Commandments
☐ **Man's Dilemma**—Romans 3:23
☐ Illustration—Flagpole

☐ ② **God Is Just** and cannot overlook our sin.
☐ **God's Standard**—Romans 6:23*a*
☐ **God's Judgment**—Matthew 25:41
☐ **Man's Destiny**—Revelation 21:8
☐ Illustration—Judge acquitting a proven murderer/brother
"Would that be justice?"

☐ ③ **God Is Loving** and has reached out to us.
☐ He has provided a way for us to be close to Him that satisfies His holy/just nature (John 3:16).
☐ **God's Son**
☐ "Who would you say Jesus is?"
God in flesh—John 1:14
☐ **God's Exchange**—Jesus becomes
☐ Our Substitute—1 Peter 3:18
☐ Our Righteousness—2 Corinthians 5:21
☐ Illustration—My record/His record chart
☐ Our Full Payment—1 John 1:7*b*; John 19:30
☐ **Man's Deliverance** from sin and its penalty —1 Corinthians 15:3–4

☐ ④ **God Is Gracious** and offers salvation as a gift.
☐ **God's Gift**—Ephesians 2:8–9
☐ **God's Offer**—John 1:12
☐ **Man's Decision**
☐ Believe—Acts 16:31
☐ Illustration—Blondine
Get in the wheelbarrow.

The Three Elements of Saving Faith

Understand
God can't tolerate or overlook my sin. He gave His life in exchange for mine and wants to give me eternal life.

Agree
I am a sinner and need a Savior.

Depend/Trust
I choose to receive Jesus' exchange—my sin and its penalty for His record and eternal life.

☐ Illustration—Two chairs
☐ Transfer dependence/trust
☐ Repent—Luke 13:5, change of mind
☐ Illustration—Point of no return
What would you do?

☐ **INVITATION**
I must offer the inquirer the gift of eternal life.

☐ ① **Ask**
☐ "Do you believe that Jesus loves you and will give you forgiveness and eternal life if you ask Him?"
☐ "Then are you willing to receive Him right now?"
☐ ② **Pray**
☐ ③ **Welcome**

☐ **ASSIMILATION**
I must call the disciple to the life of Christ.

☐ ① **Assurance**—John 5:24
☐ ② **Acceptance**—Ephesians 1:6*b*
☐ ③ **Adoption**—Romans 8:15*b*
☐ Heavenly family/Holy Spirit
☐ Church family/Church attendance
☐ ④ **Inheritance**
☐ His Victory—1 Corinthians 15:57
☐ His Life— Galatians 2:20
☐ His Word—1 Peter 2:2
☐ ***Living the Exchange:*** *A Disciple's Bible Study*

LESSON 12

GENERAL KNOWLEDGE REVIEW

I. Inviting men to come and see Jesus

When Philip found Nathanael but met resistance from him, his response was very simple, "Come and see!" Just come and meet Jesus for yourself. When you know Him like I know Him, you will love Him too.

In the parable of the wedding feast, Jesus made our soulwinning role very simple.

*Matthew 22:9—**Go** ye therefore into the highways, and as many as ye shall **find**, bid [**invite**] to the marriage.*

II. God's church growth model—Relational bridge building

GOD'S CHURCH PLANTING/GROWTH MODEL

(Each soul won and called to the life of Christ is a microcosm of planting a church.)

Conversation	λαλεω	"Spake"—Acts 11:20
Evangelization (introduction and invitation)	ευαγγελιζω	"Preaching"—Acts 11:20
Assimilation	παρακαλεω	"Exhorted"—Acts 11:23
Indoctrination (regular church involvement)	διδασκω	"Taught"—Acts 11:26

Directing a conversation to the gospel is necessary before giving the gospel is possible.

Discipleship is a man-to-man relationship that builds a man-to-God relationship. We must form a close relationship with our friend and facilitate forming close relationships in our church before we can expect him to be assimilated and experience independent growth.

III. The soulwinner's resolve

> **I resolve to direct every conversation I possibly can to the theme of themes, learn of that soul's need, and if possible meet it.**

IV. The four phases of a good gospel presentation

A. **Conversation**—We usually need to pave the way to introduce the Savior to a friend through a brief conversation that draws his heart to ours and turns his heart and mind to the gospel.

Resolve—I must turn the conversation to the theme of themes.

B. **Introduction**—Before we can expect a soul to make the decision to begin a relationship with God, it is imperative to introduce God as a person Who is knowable and has definable attributes.

Resolve—I must introduce the sinner to the Savior.

C. **Invitation**—*Giving the Exchange* will guide you to draw your friend to a decision in a direct, yet smooth, sequence that allows the Holy Spirit to convert a sinner without man's manipulation.

Resolve—I must offer the inquirer the gift of eternal life.

D. **Assimilation**—Jesus said in John 15:16, "I have chosen you . . . that ye should go and bring forth fruit, and **that your fruit should remain**." The context of this verse indicates that we are to teach our "fruit" how to abide in Christ. This portion of the presentation is only an introduction to his newly-obtained riches in Christ and is designed to encourage the new believer to plumb the depths of his inheritance by committing to study *Living the Exchange: A Disciple's Bible Study.*

Resolve—I must call the disciple to the life of Christ.

V. The priorities of *Giving the Exchange*

A. **To know Christ intimately and show Him effectively** by allowing Him to use us in His ministry of transforming lives

B. **To train men and women to be diligent, effective laborers** in the Master's plenteous harvest fields in both evangelism and discipleship

C. **To equip men and women to train others**

VI. Find Five List

Always have five people for whom you are praying and trying to befriend. To borrow a term from social networking, you need to expand your "fan base."

F—family and friends

A—associates at work or play

N—neighbors

S—strangers God brings into your path

VII. The Exchange circle of ministry

A. ***The Exchange****: An Inquirer's Bible Study*

B. ***Living the Exchange****: A Disciple's Bible Study*

C. ***Giving the Exchange****: A Course in Relational Evangelism and Discipleship*

VIII. Determined disciple-makers

Until the church utilized lay leadership in Acts 6, people were "**added** to the church," (Acts 2:47), but from that time forward "the number of the disciples **multiplied**." (Acts 6:7) God's plan to reach the world with the gospel is to utilize the man in the pew, each asking God for one soul and training that one soul to do the same, and each continuing that cycle. Review the God's Plan to Preach the Gospel to Every Creature chart.

IX. The divine-appointment concept

A. Definition: A divine appointment is when God providentially empowers you to touch a life in which He is already working.

B. There are two key elements of a divine appointment—providence and evidence.

C. Divine appointments emanate from a divine agenda.

"For the Son of man is come to seek and ***to save that which was lost****." (Luke 19:10)*

X. The biblical pattern of finding divine appointments

A. Diligently sow and reap.

B. Constantly look to the fields.

C. Consistently expect to harvest (practice the promises).

XI. The why's of *Giving the Exchange* methods

A. **The Command**

"Go ye therefore, and teach all nations, baptizing them in the name of the Father, and of the Son, and of the Holy Ghost: teaching them to observe all things whatsoever I have commanded you: and, lo, I am with you alway, even unto the end of the world. Amen." (Matthew 28:19–20)

B. **The Church**

"And he gave some, apostles; and some, prophets; and some, evangelists; and some, pastors and teachers; for the perfecting [equipping] of the saints, for [into] the work of the ministry, for the edifying of the body of Christ." (Ephesians 4:11–12)

"And the things that thou hast heard of me among many witnesses, the same commit thou to faithful men, who shall be able to teach others also." (2 Timothy 2:2)

C. **The Approach**—On the Job Training

1. Seeing the Word. Some people believe because they simply choose to believe the **words** of God and as a result *see* the **work** of God accomplished.

   Matthew 4:19—And he saith unto them, Follow me, and I will make you fishers of men.

2. Seeing the work. Others have to *see* the **works** of God before they come to faith in the **Word** of God.

It has been said that evangelism is better caught than taught.

Pacesetter—People learn best by following the example of a pacesetter and forming a close relationship with him

D. **Our Confidence**

Acts 11:21—And the hand of the Lord was with them: and a great number believed, and turned unto the Lord.

XII. Three imperatives for finding ripe fruit—John 4:35

A. "Lift up your eyes." (You may have to get your eyes off yourself first.)

B. "Look on the fields."

C. Keep looking until you find.

XIII. The art of making friends

A. The emphasis of the "Conversation" section is relationships.

B. One of the first goals of each visit is to demonstrate God's love by showing genuine interest and concern.

C. The key to being a good conversationalist is the art of asking questions.

D. Find a need and meet it. Find a hurt and heal it.

XIV. Three things about which the Holy Spirit is convicting the world—John 16:8–11

A. Sin

B. Righteousness

C. Judgment

XV. The purpose of the law

*Galatians 3:24*a—*Wherefore the law was our schoolmaster to bring us unto Christ.*

XVI. Definitions of grace and mercy

A. Grace is God's giving me what I do not deserve.

B. Mercy is God's not giving me what I do deserve.

XVII. The two necessities of the assimilation phase

A. Arrange to have your friend join you at church.

B. Motivate him to study *Living the Exchange.*

LESSON 13

ASSIGNMENT SHEET

- ☐ Complete the On the Job Training Debriefing Chart, for last week's encounters.
- ☐ Pray with your prayer partners.
- ☐ Write a letter to the person responsible for leading you to Christ to thank him or her.
- ☐ Write a testimony about how the Lord has used *Giving the Exchange* in your life. Be prepared to read it, or simply tell it in class.
- ☐ Prepare to take the One-Page Memory Sheet Exam.
- ☐ Give the entire gospel presentation without notes to someone before class.
  Have him check the points you remember, listening for accuracy. (This will serve as part of your final exam.)
- ☐ Hand out five gospel tracts.
- ☐ Pray for the lost and for God's power on your life.
- ☐ Evaluate your Find Five List, continue to actively pursue reaching the people on it, and add new people as needed.

LESSON 13

ONE-PAGE **MEMORY SHEET**

"Come and see the works of God. . . . I will declare what he hath done for my soul." (Psalm 66:5a, 16b)

☐ CONVERSATION

I must turn the conversation to the theme of themes.

☐ ① **Making Conversation**
☐ ② **Directing Conversation**
☐ "How would you describe your relationship with God?"
☐ "What do you think it takes to have a relationship with God and live with Him forever in heaven?"
☐ Personal Testimony—He has changed my life.
☐ "Are you 100% sure that all your sins are forgiven and you will go to heaven?"
☐ 1 John 5:13 or Titus 3:5
☐ "May I show you from the Bible how to have a relationship with God?"

☐ INTRODUCTION

I must introduce the sinner to the Savior.

☐ ① **God Is Holy** and cannot tolerate our sin.
☐ **God's Intolerance**—Habakkuk 1:13*a*
☐ **God's Reflection**—1 John 3:4*b*
Ten Commandments
☐ **Man's Dilemma**—Romans 3:23
☐ Illustration—Flagpole

☐ ② **God Is Just** and cannot overlook our sin.
☐ **God's Standard**—Romans 6:23*a*
☐ **God's Judgment**—Matthew 25:41
☐ **Man's Destiny**—Revelation 21:8
☐ Illustration—Judge acquitting a proven murderer/brother
"Would that be justice?"

☐ ③ **God Is Loving** and has reached out to us.
☐ He has provided a way for us to be close to Him that satisfies His holy/just nature (John 3:16).
☐ **God's Son**
☐ "Who would you say Jesus is?"
God in flesh—John 1:14
☐ **God's Exchange**—Jesus becomes
☐ Our Substitute—1 Peter 3:18
☐ Our Righteousness—2 Corinthians 5:21
☐ Illustration—My record/His record chart
☐ Our Full Payment—1 John 1:7*b*; John 19:30
☐ **Man's Deliverance** from sin and its penalty —1 Corinthians 15:3–4

☐ ④ **God Is Gracious** and offers salvation as a gift.
☐ **God's Gift**—Ephesians 2:8–9
☐ **God's Offer**—John 1:12
☐ **Man's Decision**
☐ Believe—Acts 16:31
☐ Illustration—Blondine
Get in the wheelbarrow.

> **The Three Elements of Saving Faith**
>
> **Understand**
> God can't tolerate or overlook my sin. He gave His life in exchange for mine and wants to give me eternal life.
>
> **Agree**
> I am a sinner and need a Savior.
>
> **Depend/Trust**
> I choose to receive Jesus' exchange—my sin and its penalty for His record and eternal life.

☐ Illustration—Two chairs
☐ Transfer dependence/trust
☐ Repent—Luke 13:5, change of mind
☐ Illustration—Point of no return
What would you do?

☐ INVITATION

I must offer the inquirer the gift of eternal life.

☐ ① **Ask**
☐ "Do you believe that Jesus loves you and will give you forgiveness and eternal life if you ask Him?"
☐ "Then are you willing to receive Him right now?"
☐ ② **Pray**
☐ ③ **Welcome**

☐ ASSIMILATION

I must call the disciple to the life of Christ.

☐ ① **Assurance**—John 5:24
☐ ② **Acceptance**—Ephesians 1:6*b*
☐ ③ **Adoption**—Romans 8:15*b*
☐ Heavenly family/Holy Spirit
☐ Church family/Church attendance
☐ ④ **Inheritance**
☐ His Victory—1 Corinthians 15:57
☐ His Life— Galatians 2:20
☐ His Word—1 Peter 2:2
☐ ***Living the Exchange:*** *A Disciple's Bible Study*

LESSON 13

FINAL EXAM AND TESTIMONIES

SUGGESTIONS FOR ***GIVING THE EXCHANGE*** SOULWINNING COURSE

Write any suggestions you may have to improve the *Giving the Exchange* course.

IDEAS FROM TESTIMONIES

As you listen to the testimonies of your class, record ideas that can improve your own evangelism strategies.

SECTION 4

HANDOUTS

ON THE JOB TRAINING DEBRIEFING CHART

EXPLANATION

A military unit reassembles after each exercise or foray into enemy territory to evaluate its effectiveness and make tactical changes before venturing into the next engagement with the enemy.

As important as these military debriefings are, evaluating your readiness as a soulwinner is even more important. These debriefing charts are provided to facilitate such an evaluation after each On the Job Training adventure. Make sure you retool before your next foray into enemy territory.

You will be used of God to help free captives held in the snares of the Devil. As you evaluate your effectiveness, keep in mind the **main need—God's abiding presence**. He has promised to always be with us, giving us His power to accomplish what we can never do in our own strength.

OBJECTIVE 1 DETERMINE WHERE YOU SAW GOD'S HAND IN YOUR VISITS.

How did you see God manifest Himself in your conversation?

Even when we are yielded and empowered by the Lord, we are not infallible. Certainly all of us have room to improve regarding the methods we employ while introducing others to Him. There are two more questions that will help us continue in the growth process.

OBJECTIVE 2 IDENTIFY HINDRANCES OR DISTRACTIONS THAT SHOULD BE CORRECTED.

Did you, or any of your teammates, say or do anything that hindered or distracted from the effectiveness of your conversation?

OBJECTIVE 3 IDENTIFY MEMORY LAPSES AND DISCUSS IDEAS THAT COULD HAVE FACILITATED BETTER COMMUNICATION.

Did you leave anything out of the presentation or was there anything else you could have said to better facilitate communication?

DEBRIEFING CHART

Date: ___________ Name of new friend:___________________________

OBJECTIVE 1 **Determine where you saw God's hand in your visits.**
How did you see God manifest Himself in your conversation?

____

____

OBJECTIVE 2 **Identify hindrances or distractions that should be corrected.**
Did you, or any of your teammates, say or do anything that hindered or distracted from the effectiveness of your conversation?

____

____

OBJECTIVE 3 **Identify memory lapses and discuss ideas that could have facilitated better communication**
Did you leave anything out of the presentation or was there anything else you could have said to better facilitate communication?

____

____

Date: ___________ Name of new friend:___________________________

OBJECTIVE 1 **Determine where you saw God's hand in your visits.**
How did you see God manifest Himself in your conversation?

____

____

OBJECTIVE 2 **Identify hindrances or distractions that should be corrected.**
Did you, or any of your teammates, say or do anything that hindered or distracted from the effectiveness of your conversation?

____

____

OBJECTIVE 3 **Identify memory lapses and discuss ideas that could have facilitated better communication**
Did you leave anything out of the presentation or was there anything else you could have said to better facilitate communication?

____

____

DEBRIEFING CHART

Date: ____________ Name of new friend: ________________________________

OBJECTIVE 1 **Determine where you saw God's hand in your visits.**
How did you see God manifest Himself in your conversation?

____

____

OBJECTIVE 2 **Identify hindrances or distractions that should be corrected.**
Did you, or any of your teammates, say or do anything that hindered or distracted from the effectiveness of your conversation?

____

____

OBJECTIVE 3 **Identify memory lapses and discuss ideas that could have facilitated better communication**
Did you leave anything out of the presentation or was there anything else you could have said to better facilitate communication?

____

____

Date: ____________ Name of new friend: ________________________________

OBJECTIVE 1 **Determine where you saw God's hand in your visits.**
How did you see God manifest Himself in your conversation?

____

____

OBJECTIVE 2 **Identify hindrances or distractions that should be corrected.**
Did you, or any of your teammates, say or do anything that hindered or distracted from the effectiveness of your conversation?

____

____

OBJECTIVE 3 **Identify memory lapses and discuss ideas that could have facilitated better communication**
Did you leave anything out of the presentation or was there anything else you could have said to better facilitate communication?

____

____

DEBRIEFING CHART

Date: ____________ Name of new friend: ______________________________

OBJECTIVE 1 **Determine where you saw God's hand in your visits.**
How did you see God manifest Himself in your conversation?

____

____

OBJECTIVE 2 **Identify hindrances or distractions that should be corrected.**
Did you, or any of your teammates, say or do anything that hindered or distracted from the effectiveness of your conversation?

____

____

OBJECTIVE 3 **Identify memory lapses and discuss ideas that could have facilitated better communication**
Did you leave anything out of the presentation or was there anything else you could have said to better facilitate communication?

____

____

Date: ____________ Name of new friend: ______________________________

OBJECTIVE 1 **Determine where you saw God's hand in your visits.**
How did you see God manifest Himself in your conversation?

____

____

OBJECTIVE 2 **Identify hindrances or distractions that should be corrected.**
Did you, or any of your teammates, say or do anything that hindered or distracted from the effectiveness of your conversation?

____

____

OBJECTIVE 3 **Identify memory lapses and discuss ideas that could have facilitated better communication**
Did you leave anything out of the presentation or was there anything else you could have said to better facilitate communication?

____

____

DEBRIEFING CHART

Date: ____________ Name of new friend: ______________________________

OBJECTIVE 1 **Determine where you saw God's hand in your visits.**
How did you see God manifest Himself in your conversation?

____

____

OBJECTIVE 2 **Identify hindrances or distractions that should be corrected.**
Did you, or any of your teammates, say or do anything that hindered or distracted from the effectiveness of your conversation?

____

____

OBJECTIVE 3 **Identify memory lapses and discuss ideas that could have facilitated better communication**
Did you leave anything out of the presentation or was there anything else you could have said to better facilitate communication?

____

____

Date: ____________ Name of new friend: ______________________________

OBJECTIVE 1 **Determine where you saw God's hand in your visits.**
How did you see God manifest Himself in your conversation?

____

____

OBJECTIVE 2 **Identify hindrances or distractions that should be corrected.**
Did you, or any of your teammates, say or do anything that hindered or distracted from the effectiveness of your conversation?

____

____

OBJECTIVE 3 **Identify memory lapses and discuss ideas that could have facilitated better communication**
Did you leave anything out of the presentation or was there anything else you could have said to better facilitate communication?

____

____

DEBRIEFING CHART

Date: ____________ Name of new friend:________________________________

OBJECTIVE 1 **Determine where you saw God's hand in your visits.**
How did you see God manifest Himself in your conversation?

____

____

OBJECTIVE 2 **Identify hindrances or distractions that should be corrected.**
Did you, or any of your teammates, say or do anything that hindered or distracted from the effectiveness of your conversation?

____

____

OBJECTIVE 3 **Identify memory lapses and discuss ideas that could have facilitated better communication**
Did you leave anything out of the presentation or was there anything else you could have said to better facilitate communication?

____

____

Date: ____________ Name of new friend:________________________________

OBJECTIVE 1 **Determine where you saw God's hand in your visits.**
How did you see God manifest Himself in your conversation?

____

____

OBJECTIVE 2 **Identify hindrances or distractions that should be corrected.**
Did you, or any of your teammates, say or do anything that hindered or distracted from the effectiveness of your conversation?

____

____

OBJECTIVE 3 **Identify memory lapses and discuss ideas that could have facilitated better communication**
Did you leave anything out of the presentation or was there anything else you could have said to better facilitate communication?

____

____

DEBRIEFING CHART

Date: ___________ Name of new friend: ______________________________

OBJECTIVE 1 **Determine where you saw God's hand in your visits.**
How did you see God manifest Himself in your conversation?

____

____

OBJECTIVE 2 **Identify hindrances or distractions that should be corrected.**
Did you, or any of your teammates, say or do anything that hindered or distracted from the effectiveness of your conversation?

____

____

OBJECTIVE 3 **Identify memory lapses and discuss ideas that could have facilitated better communication**
Did you leave anything out of the presentation or was there anything else you could have said to better facilitate communication?

____

____

Date: ___________ Name of new friend: ______________________________

OBJECTIVE 1 **Determine where you saw God's hand in your visits.**
How did you see God manifest Himself in your conversation?

____

____

OBJECTIVE 2 **Identify hindrances or distractions that should be corrected.**
Did you, or any of your teammates, say or do anything that hindered or distracted from the effectiveness of your conversation?

____

____

OBJECTIVE 3 **Identify memory lapses and discuss ideas that could have facilitated better communication**
Did you leave anything out of the presentation or was there anything else you could have said to better facilitate communication?

____

____

GIVING THE EXHANGE INFORMATION SHEET

WHY YOU SHOULD "GIVE THE EXCHANGE"

The Christian life is a relay race. Our faith was handed to us by those who ran before us. Now it's our turn to run, and the challenge is ours to pass the baton of faith to others. *Giving the Exchange* is a powerful resource to help mobilize believers for Great Commission living.

This thirteen-week soulwinning course will teach you to confidently present a clear, compelling gospel presentation. The classroom setting offers a sense of camaraderie as students work together to accomplish one of the greatest tasks God has given believers—soulwinning. Trainees are given weekly opportunities to do On the Job Training assisted by an experienced trainer. The trainer/trainee relationship is a perfect setting for authentic, biblical discipleship—a man-to-man relationship that builds a man-to-God relationship.

Over the course of thirteen weeks you will systematically learn a simple, but thorough, gospel outline, Scripture verses that teach each point, and illustrations that drive the truths home. The *Giving the Exchange* gospel presentation is a relational approach to soulwinning and discipleship, and trainees learn how to find and form redemptive relationships. When the first disciples inquired about Jesus, He responded, "Come and see." Later those same disciples invited friends and loved ones to "come and see" Jesus. *The Exchange* teaches the same approach—to introduce your friends to Jesus by helping them see four of His attributes: His holiness, justice, love, and grace.

The *Giving the Exchange* Gospel Presentation is integrated with two additional highly effective resources. Current American culture holds some unique challenges.

1. The postmodern mindset has robbed Americans of the biblical foundation that formerly prepared a person for salvation.
2. Few accept Christ the first time they hear the gospel presented.
3. It is difficult to assimilate new believers into church.
4. Growth seldom happens without a close mentoring relationship.

The Exchange Bible study addresses these problems. Over a four-week period an unbeliever is led to a thorough understanding of the gospel that will draw him to a decision. After having spent a minimum of four hours with a Bible-study leader discussing the most important issues of life, the two find their souls knit together, and discipleship and church attendance are most often the natural byproduct. Recently a new convert led her adult daughter to Christ using *The Exchange* Bible study. The young woman's response was typical, "What's next?"

Living the Exchange is what's next, a twelve-lesson discipleship Bible study, focusing on Spirit-empowered living that moves young believers to spiritual maturity. When you approach evangelism with discipleship in mind, the result is lasting fruit. The Exchange resources form a circle of ministry: spiritual birth → growth → productivity, resulting in potentially exponential spiritual multiplication.

What is God's plan for reaching the world? Motivated laborers! But this Great Commission work is possible only by those who are willing to depend on God's Spirit to empower them for kingdom work. "Not by might, nor by power, but by my Spirit." (Zechariah 4:6*b*) The Exchange emphasizes Spirit dependence for kingdom work.

"Eighty-two percent of people who consider themselves Christians are not involved in any kind of Kingdom service," says the Barna Research Institute. The Exchange circle of ministry addresses this problem by focusing on spiritual multiplication, not addition. You will learn to win souls, disciple them, and teach those new believers to win souls. Take the challenge to get off the sidelines and into the game. The world won't be reached by spectators. It will be reached by participants.

Please pray about participating in the *Giving the Exchange* soulwinning class.

Date for the next class: ______________________

Contacts: __________________________ __________________________

GIVING ***THE EXCHANGE***

ONE-PAGE **MEMORY SHEET**

"Come and see the works of God. . . . I will declare what he hath done for my soul." (Psalm 66:5a, 16b)

☐ CONVERSATION

I must turn the conversation to the theme of themes.

- ☐ ① **Making Conversation**
- ☐ ② **Directing Conversation**
- ☐ "How would you describe your relationship with God?"
- ☐ "What do you think it takes to have a relationship with God and live with Him forever in heaven?"
- ☐ Personal Testimony—He has changed my life.
- ☐ "Are you 100% sure that all your sins are forgiven and you will go to heaven?"
- ☐ 1 John 5:13 or Titus 3:5
- ☐ "May I show you from the Bible how to have a relationship with God?"

☐ INTRODUCTION

I must introduce the sinner to the Savior.

- ☐ ① **God Is Holy** and cannot tolerate our sin.
- ☐ **God's Intolerance**—Habakkuk 1:13*a*
- ☐ **God's Reflection**—1 John 3:4*b*
  - Ten Commandments
- ☐ **Man's Dilemma**—Romans 3:23
- ☐ Illustration—Flagpole

- ☐ ② **God Is Just** and cannot overlook our sin.
- ☐ **God's Standard**—Romans 6:23*a*
- ☐ **God's Judgment**—Matthew 25:41
- ☐ **Man's Destiny**—Revelation 21:8
- ☐ Illustration—Judge acquitting a proven murderer/brother
  - "Would that be justice?"

- ☐ ③ **God Is Loving** and has reached out to us.
- ☐ He has provided a way for us to be close to Him that satisfies His holy/just nature (John 3:16).
- ☐ **God's Son**
- ☐ "Who would you say Jesus is?"
  - God in flesh—John 1:14
- ☐ **God's Exchange**—Jesus becomes
- ☐ Our Substitute—1 Peter 3:18
- ☐ Our Righteousness—2 Corinthians 5:21
- ☐ Illustration—My record/His record chart
- ☐ Our Full Payment—1 John 1:7*b*; John 19:30
- ☐ **Man's Deliverance** from sin and its penalty —1 Corinthians 15:3–4

- ☐ ④ **God Is Gracious** and offers salvation as a gift.
- ☐ **God's Gift**—Ephesians 2:8–9
- ☐ **God's Offer**—John 1:12
- ☐ **Man's Decision**
- ☐ Believe—Acts 16:31
- ☐ Illustration—Blondine
  - Get in the wheelbarrow.

> **The Three Elements of Saving Faith**
>
> **Understand**
> God can't tolerate or overlook my sin. He gave His life in exchange for mine and wants to give me eternal life.
>
> **Agree**
> I am a sinner and need a Savior.
>
> **Depend/Trust**
> I choose to receive Jesus' exchange—my sin and its penalty for His record and eternal life.

- ☐ Illustration—Two chairs
- ☐ Transfer dependence/trust
- ☐ Repent—Luke 13:5, change of mind
- ☐ Illustration—Point of no return
  - What would you do?

☐ INVITATION

I must offer the inquirer the gift of eternal life.

- ☐ ① **Ask**
- ☐ "Do you believe that Jesus loves you and will give you forgiveness and eternal life if you ask Him?"
- ☐ "Then are you willing to receive Him right now?"
- ☐ ② **Pray**
- ☐ ③ **Welcome**

☐ ASSIMILATION

I must call the disciple to the life of Christ.

- ☐ ① **Assurance**—John 5:24
- ☐ ② **Acceptance**—Ephesians 1:6*b*
- ☐ ③ **Adoption**—Romans 8:15*b*
- ☐ Heavenly family/Holy Spirit
- ☐ Church family/Church attendance
- ☐ ④ **Inheritance**
- ☐ His Victory—1 Corinthians 15:57
- ☐ His Life— Galatians 2:20
- ☐ His Word—1 Peter 2:2
- ☐ ***Living the Exchange:*** *A Disciple's Bible Study*

MANDATORY VERSES

*"Come and see the works of God. . . . I will declare what he hath done for my soul." (Psalm 66:5*a*, 16*b*)*

1 John 5:13*a*	These things have I written . . . that ye may know that ye have eternal life.
Titus 3:5*a*	Not by works of righteousness which we have done, but according to his mercy he saved us.
Habakkuk 1:13*a*	Thou art of purer eyes than to behold evil, and canst not look on iniquity [sin].
1 John 3:4*b*	Sin is the transgression of the law.
Romans 3:23	For all have sinned, and come short of the glory of God.
Romans 6:23*a*	For the wages of sin is death.
Matthew 25:41	Then shall he say also unto them . . . Depart from me, ye cursed, into everlasting fire, prepared for the devil and his angels.
Revelation 21:8	But the fearful, and unbelieving, and the abominable, and murderers, and whoremongers, and sorcerers, and idolaters, and all liars, shall have their part in the lake which burneth with fire and brimstone: which is the second death.
John 3:16	For God so loved the world, that he gave his only begotten Son, that whosoever believeth in him should not perish, but have everlasting life.
John 1:14	And the Word [Jesus] was made flesh, and dwelt among us, (and we beheld his glory, the glory as of the only begotten of the Father,) full of grace and truth.
1 Peter 3:18*a*	For Christ also hath once suffered for sins, the just for the unjust, that he might bring us to God.
2 Corinthians 5:21	For he [God] hath made him [Jesus] to be sin for us, who knew no sin; that we might be made the righteousness of God in him.
1 John 1:7*b*	The blood of Jesus Christ his Son cleanseth us from all sin.
John 19:30*b*	"It is finished.
1 Corinthians 15:3*b*, 4*b*	Christ died for our sins . . . and . . . rose again the third day.
Ephesians 2:8–9	For by grace are ye saved through faith; and that not of yourselves: it is the gift of God: not of works, lest any man should boast.
John 1:12	But as many as received him, to them gave he power to become the sons of God, even to them that believe on his name.
Acts 16:31	And they said, Believe on the Lord Jesus Christ, and thou shalt be saved, and thy house.
Luke 13:5*b*	Except ye reprnt, ye shall all . . . perish.

GIVING ***THE EXCHANGE*** **COMMITMENT CARD**

Desiring to be the soulwinner God created me to be, I promise Him that

- I will attend the weekly training classes and On the Job Training.
- I will do all the assignments on a weekly basis.
- I will memorize the mandatory verses.
- I will memorize the *Giving the Exchange* One-Page Memory Sheet.
- By the end of the course, I will complete ten hours of soulwinning with my trainer/trainee.
- I will pray daily for the *Giving the Exchange* class, my trainer/trainee, and the lost.
- I will enlist two prayer partners and meet with them weekly to pray.
- I will pursue becoming a *Giving the Exchange* trainer.

Name: ______________________________ Date: ________________

GIVING ***THE EXCHANGE*** **PRAYER PARTNER CARD**

I agree to be a prayer partner for _________________________________.

I promise to pray

- that he/she will complete the necessary work.
- that the Lord will give his/her team weekly opportunities to present the gospel.
- that the Lord will give him/her souls for his/her labor.

I also promise to meet with him/her weekly (on the phone or in person) and pray for him/her daily.

Name: _____________________________________ Date: _____________

GIVING **THE EXCHANGE**

TRAINER'S CHECK SHEET

IN THE CAR

- ☐ Ask each team member to pray at the beginning of each On the Job Training excursion.
- ☐ Depend on Christ for boldness through the Holy Spirit. This will help instill boldness in your trainees.
- ☐ Take charge of where to go.
- ☐ Assign each team member his or her part in the visit.
- ☐ Plan when to "toss" the presentation to the trainee after Lesson 5.
- ☐ Anticipate God's divine appointments.
- ☐ Keep moving; find souls; use all the time you have.
- ☐ Use extra time in the car to practice the *Giving the Exchange* Gospel Presentation.
- ☐ Ensure spiritual conversation in the car.
- ☐ Lead a debriefing discussion that will assist in filling out the On the Job Training Debriefing Chart.
- ☐ Lead in prayer when you get back to church.

IN THE HOME

- ☐ Determine to get into homes.
- ☐ Ask, "May we come in?"
- ☐ Turn the conversation to the theme of themes and invite your new friend to "come and see the Lord."
- ☐ Use the *Giving the Exchange* Gospel Presentation.
- ☐ Use the religious questionnaires when your visits do not present an opportunity to witness.
- ☐ If you are not in a gospel presentation by 8:30, return to church.

IN THE TRAINEE'S LIFE

- ☐ Endeavor to give the trainee experience.
- ☐ Don't let a week go by without the trainee hearing or saying the presentation in person. (If necessary, go to a church member who will listen or practice the presentation with your team.)
- ☐ Remember that soulwinning is better caught than taught.
- ☐ Keep momentum going throughout the entire course, especially through the middle plateau. (Check to see if your trainee is caught up on all work and understands everything thus far.)
- ☐ *Philippians 1:6—Being confident of this very thing, that he which hath begun a good work in you will perform it until the day of Jesus Christ.*

GIVING ***THE EXCHANGE***
ON THE JOB TRAINING ORAL REPORT

The people on our team tonight were ______________________________,
______________________________, and
______________________________.

We knocked on __________ doors. We talked to __________ people. We got into __________ homes.

Our divine appointment tonight was with ______________________________.

Briefly explain why you sensed it was a divine appointment.

Briefly give the result of the visit with appropriate praise and/or prayer request.

(See the back side of this page for the rest of the report.)

GIVING ***THE EXCHANGE***
ON THE JOB TRAINING ORAL REPORT

THINGS TO REMEMBER

1. Focus on the positive things that happened while you were out, eliminating all non-essential details.
2. Keep your report brief (1–2 minutes).
3. Use first names only.
4. Fill out this form and use it as an outline for your report.

RELIGIOUS QUESTIONNAIRE

My name is _________ and this is ________ and _________. We're from ____________ Church. We're in the area doing a religion questionnaire. May we ask you eight short questions?

☐ yes ☐ no

1. According to recent studies, many Americans say they are more interested in religion today than they were earlier in life. Would you say you are more interested in spiritual things than you were five years ago? Less interested? About the same?

   ☐ more ☐ less ☐ same

2. What is your religious background?

   ☐ Baptist
   ☐ Bible church
   ☐ Catholic
   ☐ Christian Science
   ☐ Congregational
   ☐ Episcopal
   ☐ Jewish
   ☐ Lutheran
   ☐ Methodist
   ☐ Mormon
   ☐ Presbyterian
   ☐ none
   ☐ other________________

3. Do you have a church home in which you are active?

   ☐ yes ☐ no

4. How would you describe your relationship with God?

5. Do you agree with this statement? "Churches should be helping people know how to relate to God and live with Him forever in heaven."

   ☐ yes ☐ no

6. What do you think it takes to have a relationship with God and live with Him forever in heaven? (listen) Anything else?

7. Are you 100% sure that all your sins are forgiven and that you're going to heaven?

   ☐ yes ☐ no

   *1 John 5:13*a—*"These things have I written . . . that ye may know that ye have eternal life."*

   *Titus 3:5*a—*"Not by works of righteousness which we have done, but according to his mercy he saved us."*

8. May I show you from the Bible how to have a relationship with God?

   Or would you be interested in doing a four-lesson Bible study that introduces you to the God of the Bible and shows you how to have a relationship with Him?

Name____
Address____
City/State/Zip ______________________________________
Phone____
Comments ____

RELIGIOUS QUESTIONNAIRE

My name is _________ and this is ________ and _________. We're from ____________ Church. We're in the area doing a religion questionnaire. May we ask you eight short questions?

☐ yes ☐ no

1. According to recent studies, many Americans say they are more interested in religion today than they were earlier in life. Would you say you are more interested in spiritual things than you were five years ago? Less interested? About the same?

   ☐ more ☐ less ☐ same

2. What is your religious background?

   ☐ Baptist
   ☐ Bible church
   ☐ Catholic
   ☐ Christian Science
   ☐ Congregational
   ☐ Episcopal
   ☐ Jewish
   ☐ Lutheran
   ☐ Methodist
   ☐ Mormon
   ☐ Presbyterian
   ☐ none
   ☐ other________________

3. Do you have a church home in which you are active?

   ☐ yes ☐ no

4. How would you describe your relationship with God?

5. Do you agree with this statement? "Churches should be helping people know how to relate to God and live with Him forever in heaven."

   ☐ yes ☐ no

6. What do you think it takes to have a relationship with God and live with Him forever in heaven? (listen) Anything else?

7. Are you 100% sure that all your sins are forgiven and that you're going to heaven?

   ☐ yes ☐ no

   *1 John 5:13*a—*"These things have I written . . . that ye may know that ye have eternal life."*

   *Titus 3:5*a—*"Not by works of righteousness which we have done, but according to his mercy he saved us."*

8. May I show you from the Bible how to have a relationship with God?

   Or would you be interested in doing a four-lesson Bible study that introduces you to the God of the Bible and shows you how to have a relationship with Him?

Name____
Address____
City/State/Zip ______________________________________
Phone____
Comments ____